MW01141306

Speak and Win

Steven C. Hughes

Copyright 2011 Steven Hughes & Hughes Boys Media. All Rights reserved. No part of this publication may be reprinted, reproduced, transmitted, or utilized in any form or by any electronic, mechanical, or other means, now or hereafter invented, including photocopying, microfilming, and recording, or in any information retrieval system without the express written permission of Steven Hughes and Hughes Boys Media.

First Published in Canada in 2011 by Hughes Boys Media.

Trademark notice: Product or corporate names may be trademarks or registered trademarks, and are used only for identification and explanation without intent to infringe.

Author Photo: Steven Hughes copyright

Cover design by Casey Hughes

www.caseyhughes.com

ISBN: 978-0-9877728-0-0

DEDICATION

This book is dedicated to the memory of my Mother Leanne Hughes who taught me that with love for others and passion for what you do, all things are possible.

And

For Judi

Through the best of times and the darkest of hours, you have stood by my side, and I love you beyond measure.

CONTENTS

"If one advances confidently in the direction of his dreams, and endeavors to live the life which he has imagined, he will meet with a success unexpected in common hours"

Henry David Thoreau

Preface

"What we can or cannot do, what we consider possible or impossible, is rarely a function of our true capability. It is more likely a function of *our beliefs* about who we are."

Tony Robbins

Let me ask you some questions; does the thought of getting up to speak in front of other people scare you almost witless?

Do you find it hard to find the right words to convey your thoughts, or worse, do you get up to speak and draw a complete blank?

Do you get sweaty palms, butterflies, and all those other wonderful anxiety symptoms when you are in front of others speaking?

If you answered yes to any of these questions, then let me ask you this;

Do you want to learn how to create a confident and enthusiastic way to deliver presentations?

Do you want to have the skills to get up in front of people and actually enjoy the moment?

Do you want to have the audience excited to see you arrive on stage, and sorry to see you leave?

You have in your hands a book that I have created for you. The you who is afraid to deliver that speech; the you that's afraid to make that presentation, and most importantly, the you who wants to be more, and have more. So join me on this adventure, and learn how to

SPEAK AND WIN!

1

INTRODUCING PUBLIC SPEAKING

"The journey of a thousand leagues begins with a single step."

Lao Tzu

The message is a simple one: Verbal communication is a vital key to success in this new century.

Communication gives you an edge to keep abreast with the fast pace of the times. Developing your public speaking skills will greatly improve your communication skills. We all admire people who can get ideas across in a clear manner, people who speak with knowledge and passion….these are the people who excel. My question to you is; would you like to be one of these people?

The diversity of opinions today, some of which are often controversial, has increased the need for people who are skilled at public speaking. Consider that people spend 70% of their waking hours, seven days a week, communicating verbally with others. Typically a person speaks over 30,000 words per day. So let's face an inescapable fact here; people need to be able to voice their views clearly, concisely and effectively in order to function well and even prosper in society.

For some four thousand years, public speaking has been the key in building and keeping a democratic society and way of life. Its influences are vast and affect almost all aspects of life, such as the way we think or act. It is also used in court proceedings, in congress, parliament, and even in the plain setting of a classroom.

Speaking in public can sometimes be a real challenge, if not a source of embarrassment; not only to the average person, but even to persons of high rank and office, such as scholars, doctors, politicians, artists, actors and entrepreneurs. They may have hesitations in facing an audience, often accompanied by sweaty palms, stuttering, and the tip-of-the-tongue phenomenon. You will, I am sure, recall a time in your life when you were about to say something, and poof....it disappears from your mind! These dilemmas often cause untold problems to the speaker (especially in self-expression) and unpleasant effects to the audience.

You probably bought this book because you have to make a speech or presentation soon and you need valuable tips. Or perhaps you saw the link between success and effective speaking and have realized you may need help. My goal is to have this book help you achieve all this and more. I'm a good example of someone who has faced the fear and learned the skills necessary to excel at public speaking, and if you are willing to learn I can help you too.

Fact is I came from where you are. I was afraid, almost sick to my stomach every time I had to get up in school and talk. I have always been at ease talking one on one and making friends, and I had absolutely no problem socializing. My problem was when I had to present to my teachers and then later the people I worked with. I was one of those people who gets a shaky voice, sweaty palms and who wanted to be anywhere else but standing in front of those people! Then it began to dawn on me when I would watch other people giving speeches; everyone gets up there and wants to do their best. But so many people I would talk to about public speaking felt the same way I did. The people I thought were good and even great speakers shared their stories with me and you know what, hardly anyone told me they were a born speaker. I realized that almost all of us struggle with this!

When I began to focus at getting better at speaking in public I realized that sometimes the strategies that we use to help us don't work very effectively. I began to study the great speakers of our time; people like Martin Luther King, John F. Kennedy, and Winston Churchill to name but a few. I learned that they struggled just like you and I. I learned what you are about to learn; that with practice and organization you can control your fear and give insightful and compelling presentations.

There are scores of books on public speaking, but few really give practical help. This book aims to do what other books have not; I give you direct, beneficial information and easy to follow steps to help you succeed. I have assembled in the following pages the necessary tools for you to become an effective and compelling speaker. If you commit to reading *and* practicing these methods, I guarantee you that you will be speaking with confidence and getting your message across to your audience with your own unique style of public speaking!

Careful thought has also been given to people who really love to speak in public but do not have the luxury of time to prepare for such. The tips in this book will help you make your next speech a great one, and lead you to become progressively better with each succeeding speech. It aims to help people write and deliver an interesting, clear, and cogent speech quality. Technical terms or jargon in public speaking are explained here to help you grow as a public speaker. This book also adresses the questions and fears of the occasional speaker.

Included in this book is a summary of experiences in public speaking, and how they have led to success.

Aristotle said "A speaker needs three qualities – good sense, good character, and goodwill toward his hearers." Thus, public speaking is also about developing speakers, and ultimately, decent human beings.

Whether the speech is short or long, the same rules apply, like the rule of *preparation*. The habit of preparing makes good public speakers. Some would say that they speak from "inspiration," when in fact they have been preparing their speeches all their lives.

2

Public Speaking and You

"There are only two types of speakers in the world. 1. The nervous and 2. Liars."

Mark Twain

Few people are born public speakers. Hence, you are not alone when you say that you do not enjoy making speeches and presenting thoughts and ideas in front of an audience. Stage fright is inevitable. Many famous actors and musicians are always nervous to a certain degree before every play or performance. Many credit these nerves with their ability to deliver amazing performances.

Now I am sure that at one time or another you have heard a public speaking horror story about someone's friends, family, or co-workers. It's easy to find stories about the "crash and burn" moments that happen in Public Speaking, despite the fact most people want to forget about it! The story I am about to recount happened to me; I was the public speaker, I was up there on the stage, and I had to make a very fast decision in a very embarrassing situation.

I was on stage, ready to deliver a presentation on lighting techniques for small stage areas to a group of student stage directors. I greeted the group, all 60 of them, and began my presentation. All was going as planned.

As I was beginning to move about the stage illustrating the placement of the lights and the effect it would have on the object or person being lit, I dropped the prop I was holding. As I bent down to pick it up, I heard the ominous (and loud) sound of a pant seam letting go. That's right, it was THAT seam....!

So, here I am up on stage, with my backside exposed to all. In an effort to save some embarrassment, I spent the remainder of the presentation doing a Crab walk back and forth across the stage in a vain attempt to limit my "exposure"!

I told you that story to let you know that things like this can, and in my case did happen, but it's not the end. Your first experience with public speaking might not turn out the way you had hoped for. You may even consider it to be a complete failure in your own eyes. But by my experience that is simply not the case.

There is nothing wrong or unusual about being nervous while speaking in front of people. The author Jacob Braude summed it up when he said "The brain is a remarkable thing. It starts to function the instant you are born and doesn't stop until the moment you get up to speak."

So even though some people feel that getting up in front of an audience can seem like going in front of the firing squad, learning to speak effectively with a goal to move and influence your audience can be a hugely satisfying experience for you.

Perhaps you think your career does not require public speaking. Well, this is where you're wrong, because no matter what your job is, public speaking will ultimately come into the picture. Studies have shown time and again that the ability to communicate effectively in any job is the number one skill prized by managers and business owners. Therefore, this chapter focuses on the specifics of the communication process and the significance of public speaking in our daily lives.

"If all my possessions were taken from me with one exception, I would choose to keep the power of speech, for by it I would regain the rest"

Daniel Webster

Four General Types of Public Speakers

CATEGORY	CHARACTERISTICS
The Avoider	*Does everything possible to avoid facing an audience.* In some cases, avoiders seek careers that do not involve making presentations.
The Resister	*Becomes fearful when asked to speak.* This fear may be strong. Resisters may not love to speak in public, but they have no choice. When they speak, they do so with great reluctance.
The Accepter	*Capable of doing presentations but is not that enthusiastic to do them.* Accepters occasionally give presentations and feel good about them. Occasionally the presentations can be quite persuasive, and satisfying.
The Seeker	*Always looks for opportunities to speak.* Seekers understand that anxiety can be a stimulant that fuels enthusiasm during presentation. Seekers work hard at building their professional communication skills and self-confidence by speaking often.

What Roles Can Public Speaking Play in Your Life?

Success in public speaking can open a whole world of opportunities for you. It can help you conquer new frontiers. It can broaden your horizons through personal development, influence, and advances in your profession. You will read this time and again in this book, you will hear me say it when I speak to audiences large and small, and should we ever work together one on one, you will hear it again: the ability to communicate effectively is the defining ability of leaders. It is the one thing that can create opportunity for you, the one thing that can send your career and dreams in an upward spiral. This applies if you are in the mailroom, pumping gas, serving customers in a store, or sitting behind the president's desk. When you learn to communicate effectively, you learn to lead yourself and others to new opportunities!

1. Public Speaking Improves Your Personal Development

In noted researcher and author Abraham Maslow's hierarchy of needs, realizing a person's self-worth ranks the highest. Giving speeches helps the speaker realize self-worth through the personal satisfaction they experience whenever a good speech is given. The speaker becomes more confident, especially when the audience responds positively. The positive reaction received after your public speaking event can reduce future anxiety when you are asked by someone to speak in front of people again.

I know of a student who dropped out of numerous courses because he hated speaking in front of the class. But, after taking the time to read as many books on public speaking as he could lay his hands on, studying and practicing the techniques on how to build up his confidence, he decided to give public speaking another chance, and was successful. In fact, he came to enjoy the experience and even volunteered to give more speeches. This is the attitude that leads to success not only in delivering compelling speeches and presentations, but in creating success in other aspects of your life.

Through the tools I outline in this book, tools like research, conceptualization, and organization, you will have a systematic and effective way of presenting your ideas and you will be able to express yourself better. You will also become more open to other people. Everyone knows what it's like to be the stranger in the room; you don't know anyone, you are nervous about approaching another person or group in the room, because you don't know how to present yourself and communicate effectively. Simply put, you lack the self assuredness to approach this new situation with confidence.

Learning the skills associated with effective public speaking helps you build confidence to approach new situations like this as an opportunity; it's an opportunity to start communicating with new people and learn new things. Furthermore, speaking skills put you in a more significant role as you talk with people of high standing. Many people have seen their career fortunes skyrocket as a result of giving a compelling speech or presentation to the right people at the right time. I know this from personal experience, as my career began to rapidly advance when I began speaking with confidence. I tell you this from my personal experience: there is nothing quite like the feeling you get after delivering a speech or giving a presentation, and the audience reacts with heartfelt applause. This response from the audience is a direct reflection of your level of communication skills and acumen. Developing these skills provides a major contribution to your self-esteem and personal development.

2. Public Speaking Influences Your Society

It is not only you who can benefit from the art of communication but society as well. Most governments heed the voice of their citizens; with proper communication skills, you can represent the public in voicing out your rights and opinions. A few years ago I began taking a stand against some of the actions of the city administration in the small suburban city I live in, when it became apparent that they were not always working in the best interests of the citizens who elected them. Through a well crafted letter writing campaign and appearances at the city council chambers, momentum was created that led to an administration change in the next election. While I did not work alone in orchestrating these changes, I spoke and delivered passionate speeches which supported the change. When I spoke out, I made my voice heard to all who cared to listen. Speaking up and out is at the heart of communication, and is the heart of democracy.

One excellent way to help you develop your presentation skills and serve your community is to serve as a volunteer on a committee, or as a member of a community charity. Usually when a neighborhood committee holds regular meetings, it discusses certain issues or courses of action. In the discussions, various opinions are expressed and there you will have an opportunity to engage in the interplay of public speaking. Participation will expose you to different styles of communication, different ways to present information, and help you involve yourself at your own pace.

People from all walks of life need to speak in public, whether formally or otherwise. From kids reciting in school, to folks in a town meeting, to citizens voicing out national issues; from a plain market vendor, to a president of a company. There is really **no** way you can avoid public speaking, and I think by the end of this book you'll be saying, "Why would I want to?"

"Why not go out on a limb? That's where the fruit is."

Will Rogers

3. Public Speaking Advances Your Profession

Consider this: surveys time and again show that the number one job of people in business is to communicate effectively. Those who have careers with an upward track are those who can get their message across. Those who lack the confidence and skills to communicate well are, to be blunt, doomed to languish in low paying jobs with little advancement. As a writer, researcher, and sales and public speaking trainer, I read extensively. Many of the books I read are biographies of successful women and men. Time and time again, they note that their ability to communicate critical ideas, concepts and plans has been the defining skill that shaped their careers. So it goes almost without saying that public speaking can help in your career, and eventually, your finances. Sometimes success is gauged by answers to questions like, "How long have you been in your job?" or "Do you hold an MBA degree or something similar?" However, research has concluded that one of the best indicators of success in any profession is whether the person is sometimes asked to give speeches. Those who give more speeches tend to have higher salaries than those who give less or no speeches.

Let's take Sarah. She is a competent, average architect, in a company of about 300 people. She enrolls in a public speaking seminar that teaches two hours a week for six weeks. After two months, and with Sarah taking the time to seek out opportunities to engage in presentations to her colleagues, she is promoted to senior architect! Her managers have been noticing her superb presentations, and the ease with which she relays often complex information to her colleagues and clients. Fictional story, yes. Fictional results? I don't think so.

The longer you work for an organization and the higher you climb the organizational ladder, the more your manager will ask you to preside over meetings and to give talks to staff and subordinates or clients. The higher your position, the greater your responsibility to lead people under you; and the more you must speak effectively. A manager once said to me, "From the chairman of the board to the assistant manager of the most obscure department in this company, nearly everyone in our business speaks in public or makes a speech at some time or the other."

Aside from big organizations like IBM and General Motors, small organizations and businesses in the country also need workers who are good public speakers. Take the high school coach, for example. If he is not persuasive enough to tell the school board that new gym equipment is needed, the school athletes might have to bear with the old gym equipment. If they are not equally persuasive in helping motivate the players, they will have no need for that new equipment!

In the same way, if parents are not convincing enough when they complain about a school dress code, their children may end up still wearing random clothing, rather than nice uniforms in school. If salespeople cannot explain their products with a convincing sales pitch, then fewer people would buy their products. This is also true for nurses, doctors, firemen, police personnel and other professions. Even employees of General Motors meet regularly to make group decisions that they will present formally to CEO level management teams.

The bottom line is this: Whichever road you take, you will encounter instances that require you to communicate with groups of people or speak in public; and by now you should be starting to get my message- learn to master these skills, and you can be, do, or have virtually anything you want!

3

GETTING STARTED: YOUR FIRST SPEECH

"It usually takes me more than three weeks to prepare a good impromptu speech"

Mark Twain

Imagine you're sitting in a classroom. Who do you think delivers excellent speeches? You may select those who look smart or those who often recite in class. You may think that these people are actually more confident than you think they are. Or perhaps, they are born speakers and you are not.

Well, it may surprise you that they're probably thinking the same thing about you! They may also feel that you are a born speaker and envy you because they have fears in public speaking. Some may have special interests in public speaking, but most people do not know anything about it because they have always lacked the nerve to stand and be heard.

Then again, you may actually be a good speaker without realizing it. It pays to find out by visualizing yourself doing it, and then actually doing it. You may be just like this student during his first speech in class.

Dave needed to prepare a long speech. Two weeks before, he had started writing his speech. He could not sleep at night. In fact, the night before his speech, he did not sleep at all. However, when he finally did his speech and saw it on video, he realized that it was not as bad as he expected it to be. Dave did not experience the usual symptoms of speech anxiety, such as going blank while speaking, or speaking very softly and hearing chuckles in the audience. Through the video, Dave discovered that he has actually improved his public speaking.

Preparing Yourself to Speak

"Failures don't plan to fail, they fail to plan"

Harvey McKay

Here are the basic rules of public speaking:

- ***Gain an understanding of who you are.*** Discover your own knowledge, capabilities, biases and potentials. The best public speakers are those who have a passion for what they are speaking about. Discover what interests you. What do you love talking about? Perhaps it's a hobby, sports, or your career? When you take the time to find what you would love to tell others about, you will speak with passion, and those to whom you are speaking will pick up on the passion.

Gain an understanding of your audience. Ponder upon what the audience wants to hear, what provokes their interest, what they believe in and what they want to know. One of the biggest reasons for a speaker's failure is that they have not taken the time to learn what their audience's "hot buttons" are. A hot button is the thing that is going to get this audience leaning forward in their seats and hanging on your every word. Ask yourself the W5-

- **WHO** is the audience?
- **WHY** are these people in the audience?
- **WHEN** do they expect to use what I am telling them?
- **WHERE** can my words make the biggest impact?
- **WHAT** do they expect from me, the speaker?

- ***Gain an understanding of the situation.*** Consider how the setting of the place and other unforeseen factors could affect the way you deliver your speech. Picture this, you have taken the time to write your presentation, to rehearse it time and time again, to work out all of the problem areas, and here you are in the auditorium or conference room ready to go. You step up to the podium, adjust the microphone, start to speak and NOTHING! Your microphone is dead. No one can hear you. People are saying "speak up….we can't hear you….what did she say?.... You need to take control over having the room you are presenting in set up and functional BEFORE you do your presentation. And by before, I don't mean 5 minutes before.

I make a point of visiting the facility that I am scheduled to speak at a day or two before my presentation. I have a check list I work from, that details the following: Who is in charge of setting up the room (I want to meet them and introduce myself), where are the lighting controls, where are the heating controls, where are the audio visual controls, what is the set up schedule? You basically want to eliminate as many of the issues that could cause you any potential problems BEFORE they occur. Yes, I know that things happen, sometimes they are out of our control, but frankly most problems come about as a result of poor planning. Don't let this happen to you. PLAN for success, and don't allow a lack of attention to the details derail your presentation! See my web site at **www.speakandwin.com** to download a free pre-event checklist; it is a must do for anyone serious about successful presentations!

- **_Anticipate the response from the audience._** Make sure you have a clear purpose in mind so that the audience will respond in the way you want them to. If you know the bias of your audience, you will have a much better idea of how they will respond to your presentation. Understand also what the expected response is. In other words, if you are talking to a group of pensioners about your company reducing their pension income, what do you think that response will be? If you are talking to a group of youths about the pending closure of a favorite park, what will their response be? Culture, age, political affiliation....all of these factors can play into audience response to your message. So plan your presentation to create the appropriate response from your audience.

- **_Search for other sources of information._** There might be more materials available for you to make your speech more colorful. You will notice throughout this book that I use quotations frequently. I do this because these quotations tie into the point I am going to be making. Quotes can act as anchor points for you and your audience.

People often remember quotes long after hearing the presentation. And please, be very careful about boring people to near death with an endless stream of PowerPoint slides, pie charts, graphs and other stupor inducing materials. There is no quicker way to put an audience to sleep than by putting them in a warm room, turning the lights down, and putting on slide after slide. If you are going this way with your presentation, you might as well bring blankets and teddy bears to hand out at the door! Keep your information current, topical, and even a bit edgy; this will help keep the audience engaged!

- *Come up with an argument that is reasonable.* Make sure that the purpose of your speech is supported by clear and reliable data to formulate a sound argument. As noted above in the point on searching for other sources of information, present data that supports your position, is accurate and truthful, persuades the audience and achieves your desired outcome.

- *Add structure to your message.* Organize your ideas so that the audience will have an easy time following and digesting your ideas. There have been countless times when I have attended lectures or presentations where the person presenting bounces from point to point in a seemingly random pattern. Do this and you will lose your audience! There is an old saying, "God is in the details". In our context here, take this to mean that you must have a detailed plan of how your presentation is going to progress from point to point. You need flow, and you gain flow by creating a structure to your presentation. Remember, everything in life has a beginning, a middle, and an end. Plan accordingly!

- ***Talk directly to your audience.*** Make sure the language you are using is one that your audience is comfortable with. Consider the occasion in delivering your speech. If you are speaking to a younger audience, it may well be appropriate to include common speech elements that this age demographic uses. For example, telling your 10 to 30 year old audience that you read a friend's email or text and it made you LOL will mean something to them, and nothing to your 60-80 year old audience. Obviously profanity is not recommended while speaking to any age group. It is simply in bad taste, and even as a "shock value" tool it really has little value. Avoid it!

- ***Gain self-confidence through practice.*** When you are attending one of my seminars or listening to one of my audio presentations you will hear me repeat the following: It is _only_ through practice that you can effectively present your speech. Master the flow of your presentation by repeatedly rehearsing it. That way, you can have command over your speech. The best speakers and actors in the world rehearse, and rehearse more. That's how they create the flow that makes them successful actors and sought after speakers.

Becoming a Good Public Speaker

"There are certain things in which mediocrity is not to be endured, such as poetry, music, painting, public speaking."

Jean de la Bruyere

You have probably heard professors give boring and monotonous lectures. Dull presentations clearly point out that a lot of people do not give much importance to good speeches. These speakers may even be unaware that they are boring or ineffective because they lack knowledge about the basic characteristics of a good speech. To prevent this pitfall, you must remember some basic principles.

1. Respect the variety of the audience.

Good speakers do not look down on their audience. They consider the audience as equals. They know that the listeners have different backgrounds, hence communicating to each of them effectively would also entail different methods.

Before actually organizing a speech, you have to take into consideration your audience. Again, consider such things as age, gender, and cultural backgrounds. What do they know about your topic? What are their beliefs and values? By looking at these factors, you can choose a topic that suits them and style your speech in the way you feel would be most effective.

The whole experience can be more enjoyable if you prepare well for the individual and cultural differences of your audience. For example, will both male and female listeners appreciate the information you will prepare? Would your Asian audience be comfortable with the language you're using as much as the Native Americans would? Would some of your comments offend the senior citizens while addressing the younger generation? The more you know about the audience, the better the chances are that you will capture their attention, and the more you can make your speech fit their situations. Further, by taking the time to understand the demographic of your audience, you will find the chances of delivering an impactful message are greatly increased, as they would feel comfortable listening to you and you would have a better interaction with them.

2. Know as much as possible about listening.

A successful outcome for a speech not only depends on good speakers it depends on good listeners as well. It's a two-way process. If the speaker prepares a very polished speech, it would be wasted if the audience didn't listen. Also, you need to know how to "listen" to the gesticulated reactions of your audience. How comfortable or uneasy they look speaks volumes in terms of their interest or comprehension. Very few people listen with complete attention to what they are hearing. There are a multitude of distractions, the room is too cold, it's too hot, I wonder what's for lunch, why did I choose this outfit today….the list goes on and on. The human mind processes words at a rate of about 500 words per minute, and the problem is that we speak at about 150 words per minute. So this is leaving lots of time for your audience's minds to wander off in all directions!

Most listeners are taking in what they hear, comparing it against their core beliefs, and deciding if they will accept or reject the idea, thought or premise that you are presenting. At the same time this is happening, they are also judging you. Does this person know what they are talking about? Why are they saying this to me? What experience do they have to be able to talk to me about this? And why did they choose *that* suit?

Now at this point you may be wondering if there is any logical reason for you to even attempt to speak, if no one is listening to you. But let's face it, if you don't speak, how do you communicate? How do you do a sales call, deliver an idea, ask for a raise, or encourage someone to do what you want them to do?

The answer?

When you are face to face with the people you are speaking to, you have a measure of control. You can learn to read your audience, and to understand how they are listening to you. Are they sitting there, looking around the room, at the floor, the ceiling? Or are they sitting upright, eyes focused on you? Or forward, leaning in towards you, hanging on your next word?

As a speaker, you have the flexibility to adjust your message for your audience. You can draw from common experience. For example, if you are an armed forces veteran, and are addressing other veterans, you have a common ground. Look for these "common ground" situations, and use them to your advantage when delivering your message.

This is a very powerful tool, and really is the core to engaging your audience. Most of the presentations you will give are related to topics that are of interest to you, and as a result you are more likely to have a common ground with your audience.

3. Organize carefully to improve understanding and recall.

The best presentations are those with interconnected ideas that flow smoothly from one idea to the next. It is effective because the listeners will be able to follow your arguments and will not get confused along the way.

Three parts of a well-organized speech:

- ***Introduction:*** Capture the attention of your audience, boost their interest, and give them a background of your topic. Start with a bold statement, and then fill in the blanks. You need to make sure your audience knows why the presentation or speech you are about to give is important. Look at it from their perspective. As the listener, what is the benefit to them? Focus your introduction on the audience, and how your speech or presentation will benefit them. This will start you off on the right foot!
- ***Body:*** Start with your main ideas. Keep them organized and support them with visual and

verbal aids as much as possible. But do be careful not to let your visuals overwhelm your words. I prefer to keep my visuals lean, brief and to the point. It is best to let your words draw visuals in the minds of the audience. Think of the old saying, "A picture is worth a thousand words". Now make it your goal to have your words painting the most fascinating pictures in the minds of your audience.

- **_Conclusion:_** Provide a recap of all your points and join them together in a way that will create an impact on your listeners, making them remember your points. Don't let the ending of your talk be a surprise to the audience. Towards the conclusion, pause, lower your tone, perhaps say "now that I have finished my speech / presentation", or use the phrase, "in conclusion", or "to sum up". Be sure that you summarize what you have been saying through your presentation. Remember what I wrote earlier- the brain can process up to 500 words per minute, and at best, unless you are an auctioneer at work, you can deliver about 150 words per minute. So odds are the audience members have not been there mentally for your entire presentation. There is a saying regarding presentations, and it's "tell them what you're going to tell them, tell them, and then tell them what you told them."

Take the time to briefly summarize your key points, and your "take aways"- the things you really want the audience to take from your presentation. If the purpose of your talk has been to motivate your audience to do something, be something, or buy something, now is the time to "close the sale", and ask them to take action on your request.

4. Use language effectively.

Keep it short. The simpler the language you use, the more powerful and interesting your speech will be; don't use a $5 word when a $1 word will work just as well. Too many words expressing a single idea will only confuse the audience and will make your argument weak. By keeping it short but accurate, your audience will remember what you say and they will appreciate it.

5. Sound natural and enthusiastic.

The problem with first timers is they either memorize the speech verbatim or rely on too many flashcards for their notes. These can make the speaker sound unnatural. Talk normally to people so they will listen more to you. By being natural and enthusiastic, it will be like discussing a favorite subject with your friends. Basically, avoid putting up a "speaking disguise" when you talk. Treat it like an ordinary conversation with your usual companions. Be it 5 people or 50,000, when I get up to speak, I consider myself to be having a conversation with each and every person that is in the room. By thinking of your presentations in this way you are taking a huge amount of stress off yourself, and you are more able to act and feel natural.

6. Use high-quality visual aids.

A simple text containing key phrases and pictures is an example of a visual aid. Usually, visual aids (Chapter 10) can be anything that supplements your speech. It will greatly help your listeners to follow the flow of your ideas and to understand them at a faster rate. It also gives credibility to your speech, which makes you feel more relaxed and confident throughout. However, avoid using poor visuals because they become more of a confusing distraction and do not support you. Poorly made visual aids also show a disregard for the audience, as people will assume you could not be bothered to take the time to produce something of quality to present to them. Treat all of your visual preparations with as much importance as the speech preparation itself. If you are not already proficient in the use of Microsoft PowerPoint, you need to be. In many organizations it is the tool of choice for presentations. It can seem a bit daunting to use at first, but once you create a few practice slides you will do fine.

But please remember; don't go overboard with the special effects...keep it simple and to the point.

7. Give only ethical speeches.

Accuracy is very important. It would be difficult for your audience to make informed choices if the information you give is false or vague. Do your research to ensure credibility and clarity in everything that you plan to say and in all of your visual tools. Avoid plagiarism, falsification and exaggeration of your information. Also, when trying to persuade, do not manipulate, deceive, force, or pressure. Develop good arguments through sound logic and concrete evidence. This is ethical persuasion. Once information is exaggerated, it becomes unethical because it prevents listeners from making informed choices. Realize too that you will frequently be speaking on topics that your audience has at least a passing knowledge of. It is your duty as a speaker and presenter to ensure that the information you are conveying is accurate, or you will face very difficult questions, or worse, a hostile audience.

Basically, good speakers aim to change the beliefs, values, or attitudes of the audience through clean and thoroughly considered persuasion techniques.

Use your visual tools to create speaking success:

- Use your facial expressions to convey your passion, use eye contact, gestures and avoid nervous traits like hand wringing, pacing and hanging onto the podium for dear life!

- Get involved with your listeners. React and interact with them to keep their interest and minds focused on you and your message. If the audience is staring at the ceiling, you are doing something wrong, not them. The time to correct this is NOW. Have ready in your presentation several statements, observations, and maybe even an appropriate humorous anticdote to draw the audience back to you.

- Use your visual tools. Handouts and PowerPoint are great ways to keep the audience's attention on the topic. Just don't make these tools the focus of your presentation. Remember they likely did not come to sit in the dark and read; they want to hear what you have to say as well.

- Most of all speak with enthusiasm, be sincere, and be animated when you speak! Be excited to be there at that moment. Create your content in anticipation of presenting something that you feel thrilled to be talking about.

4

DEVELOPING SPEAKER CONFIDENCE

"According to most studies, people's number one fear is public speaking. Number two is death. Death is number two. Does that sound right? This means to the average person, if you go to a funeral, you're better off in the casket than doing the eulogy."

Jerry Seinfeld

No matter how interested and experienced we may be at public speaking, anxiety cannot be avoided. We experience it especially as the day of the speech gets closer. We start to ask questions that make our stomachs churn. For example: Will the audience like me? Will my mind go blank when I begin to speak? Have I prepared adequately?

If the thought of delivering a speech makes you nervous, you are not alone! According to a commonly quoted survey, more people are afraid of public speaking than they are of dying. People who experience a high level of apprehension while speaking are at a great disadvantage compared to more conversational, confident people.

Individuals who confidently express themselves are viewed as more competent. They also create a better impression during job interviews and are more likely to be promoted than apprehensive people.

Confidence develops a positive impression while anxiety creates a negative one. When we speak, we are communicating in three ways - verbally, visually, and vocally. Our verbal delivery may be clear and well organized, but when we are anxious, the audience will likely notice more our negative vocal and visual signs (for example, lack of eye contact, poor posture, hesitant delivery, and strained vocal quality). Yet, when we are confident and our verbal, visual, and vocal signals are in unity, we look more credible.

The key is practice, practice, practice! It may appear that people who deliver effective speeches and presentations are doing so with little effort, but the opposite is true. What you are seeing is the culmination of a weeks, months, and perhaps years of practice. Years ago I had the pleasure of talking to the actress Cloris Leachman after she taught a class at the acting school I was attending, and when I asked her how she could deliver lines in her flawless style she looked at me and said, "kid, you need to read the line, feel what the line means to your character, then say the line with all the passion you feel that character should have. That's how you become an actor".

If we want people to believe us when we speak, if we want to improve the impressions we make, we need to boost our passion for the topic, not just the words. This is why I have stressed at other points in this book that you must find a point of passion in what you are presenting. If it helps you, look at it through the audience's eyes. What would excite you about the topic if you were sitting there? Develop this skill, and from this will flow confidence. This chapter will give you some tips on how to manage speech anxiety to give more confident and professional deliveries.

Call it speech anxiety, stage fright, or communication apprehension; you have to understand it for numerous reasons. First, speech anxiety can incapacitate you. Second, misconceptions about it can strengthen your anxiety. Finally, knowing the strategies for managing speech anxiety can help lessen your apprehension.

Factors Contributing to Speech Anxiety

Speech anxiety is not new – it's been around for as long as people have been talking to one another. Most speakers who have experienced speech anxiety have learned the hard way about the importance of being calm and confident when speaking.

Some feel nervous while others stay calm and relaxed when speaking. Factors in speech anxiety differ from person to person, but general factors apply to all of us.

Knowing the causes of speech anxiety is the first step in managing it effectively. Many anxiety-generating factors affect nearly all of us, including:

- Poor preparation
- Inappropriate self-expectations
- Fear of evaluation
- Excessive self-focusing
- Fear of the audience
- Not understanding our body's reactions

Misconceptions about Speech Anxiety

I doubt that anyone would say that experiencing speech anxiety is enjoyable. However when we better recognize why our bodies respond as they do, we become more prepared to face our anxieties. Let us examine some misconceptions and how to counter them.

Myth / Misconception	Reality
1. Everyone will know if a speaker has speech anxiety.	Few, if any, will notice. So keep the secret to yourself and start acting confident.
2. Speech anxiety will intensify as the speech progresses.	It's all up to you. Mostly, a well-prepared speaker will relax as the speech progresses.
3. Speech anxiety will ruin the effect of the speech.	If you let it, it will. On the contrary, a small amount of speech anxiety may improve a speaker's effectiveness.
4. The audience is inherently hostile and will be overly critical of what we do.	Most listeners are polite, especially when the speaker is obviously trying to do well.

Strategies for Managing Speech Anxiety

Every speaker has to know the different strategies available for managing speech anxiety. As you give speeches, you learn strategies that work specifically for you. Let's look at some strategies that have been very effective for many speakers.

1. Be Well-Prepared and Practice Your Speech.

Nothing can make you feel more anxious than knowing that you are not well prepared. After all, isn't your anxiety all about looking stupid in the eyes of your audience? Poor preparation will guarantee this result!

To prepare adequately, first make sure you know your listeners beforehand and organize your speech and visual aids for this specific group. The internet is a very valuable tool in gathering information on your audience, especially if they are an organized group. Do your research!

Next, prepare easy-to-follow notes. Using these notes, practice your speech three or more times from start to end speaking out louder each time. Remember also my tip on recording yourself with a video camera; this will help identify the points in your speech that are causing you problems. Mentally thinking through your speech is not the same thing as actually speaking in front of the audience. For instance, if you will be standing during your speech, stand while practicing. If you will be using visual aids, practice using them. As you practice, time yourself to check if you have to shorten or lengthen the speech. Time management of your presentation is critical; you do not want to have to rush through the last 10 minutes of your presentation in 6 minutes!

Lastly, consider all possible questions and prepare answers for them. Knowing that you are well prepared will help lessen much of your apprehension. If you have a firm understanding of your topic, you will have a good idea of the potential questions that will be asked. If you get a question that you cannot answer, or one that is too long to respond to in the amount of time you have allotted for your Q & A session, tell the person asking the question that given your allotted time, you would not have the time to respond properly, and ask them to join you after the presentation so you can give them a detailed response. I don't usually have any issues from the audience with this response, as I am sincere when I make this statement, and ensure that I seek that person out to answer their question thoroughly.

2. Warm Up First.

Speakers are no different from singers who warm up their voices, musicians who warm up their fingers, or athletes who warm up their muscles before a performance. Before giving a speech, make it a goal to set aside a minimum of ten to twelve minutes for vocal warm ups in a private and quiet area before you take the stage. Just like me, I'm sure you'll find it works great for focusing, relaxing and settling any nerves!

Various techniques can help you do these warm ups. For instance, try singing up and down the scale, the way singers do before a concert. Read aloud a note or a page from a book, changing your volume, pitch, rate, and quality. Try some good old fashioned limericks (remember she sells sea shells by the seashore?).

Do some stretching exercises such as touching your toes and rolling your head from side to side. Practice different gestures such as pointing, pounding your fist, or shrugging your shoulders. Just like musicians and athletes, these warm-up exercises will help you relax and will make sure that you are prepared to present at your very best.

3. Use Deep Breathing.

To ease the tension that you are feeling, and give yourself a health and energy boost, begin by sitting or lying in a comfortable position. Breathe in slowly and deeply through your nose, counting to five. Hold your breath while slowly counting to five. Exhale slowly through your mouth, slowly counting to nine. Try to expel as much air as possible from your lungs.

It is important to concentrate on counting and your breath. As you breathe in, feel you lungs fill up with fresh air. Focus on your heart, and feel your heart rate slow. By exhaling as deeply as you can, you cleanse all the stale air held in your lungs. Repeat this several times, and you will feel the relaxation deep breathing brings.

Tension buster deep belly breathing exercise:

Breathe in deeply through your nose, but instead of expanding your chest, expand your belly. Feel the immediate relaxation.

Focus on the pause in your breath.

When you breathe in and out there are two slight pauses in the process. Breathe in, take a slight pause, breathe out, and take another slight pause. Focus your attention on these pauses. Just by focusing on these pauses, you will feel your breath as it becomes deeper and slower.

As you exhale, think that the pressure and nervousness are slowly draining down your arms and out your fingertips, and down your body and legs and out your toes.

Repeat the procedure a second or third time if necessary.

Personally, I visualize myself as a tree, with all of the stress cascading down my trunk, through my roots, and deep into the ground. Hey....it works for me!

4. Prepare an Introduction That Will Relax You and Your Audience.

Most speakers find that once they get a favorable audience reaction, they will relax. This is why some speakers begin with humor – it relaxes them and their audience. I always consider that the safest target for humor is me. It shows your audience that you can laugh at yourself, and it makes them feel less self conscious. If a humorous introduction is improper or you are uncomfortable with humor, sharing a personal experience is another alternative. Try using a shared experience. For example, I will occasionally open by telling about the airline losing my bag, and having to scramble to find something to wear. Or maybe I could not find a parking spot and had to run four blocks to make it on time. Most people can relate, and it usually breaks the ice with the audience. Whatever you prefer, develop your opening so you can feel comfortable throughout your speech.

5. Focus on Meaning.

Rather than worrying about how you look or sound, or about whether you are impressing your listeners, focus your energy on getting your meaning across to your audience. In other words, be sure your listeners are following the order of your speech and understanding your ideas. Pay close attention to their nonverbal feedback. If they look confused, explain the concept again or add another example. A speaker who is focusing on the needs of their audience soon forgets about being anxious.

6. Use Visual Aids.

Visual aids (Chapter 10) make listening easier for your audience and increase your confidence as a speaker. They make it practically impossible for you to forget your main points. If you're unsure of the next point, just put up your next visual aid. Moreover, using visual aids such as posters, flipcharts, or actual objects not only can add eye-catching movements to your presentation, but can also keep you fully engaged in your presentation, so you'll be bothered less by other non consequential details and distractions.

7. Develop a Positive Mental Attitude.

With positive imagery, you develop a positive, vivid, and detailed mental image of yourself. When you visualize yourself speaking confidently, you become more confident. In your mind, you can simulate feelings (of pride, for instance) even when no real situation exists. Obviously, positive imagery alone will not give you the outcome you want unless you prepare and practice your speech.

Positive self-imagery can be used in every aspect of life. It helps us manage apprehension in job interviews, problem-solving discussions, testing situations, or any circumstances in which our confidence needs a boost.

To succeed in public speaking, you have to visualize yourself as a successful speaker. No amount of talk, encouragement, or practice will make you successful if you deem yourself an anxious or ineffective speaker.

"We may affirm absolutely that nothing great in the world has been accomplished without passion"

Georg Wilhelm Friedrich Hegel

5

OVERCOMING YOUR FEAR

"All of our dreams can come true if we have the courage to pursue them."

Walt Disney

Would you be surprised if someone told you that, of all of the phobias known to man, that topophobia, most commonly known as "stage fright", is the #1 fear?

Symptoms of topophobia include intense anxiety, rapid heartbeat, blushing, a "dread" feeling, prickly or sweaty skin, cold hands and / or feet, a fear of speaking and an aversion to eye contact with anyone. Some believe it to be caused by a past perhaps unrelated traumatic experience that has latched onto a situation, in effect rewiring the brain to associate that fear with a public speaking situation.

Left unexplored, this fear is a real life wrecker, as it can derail your career, your success with the opposite sex, and leave you feeling helpless to overcome it.

You will benefit at the beginning of your speech if you free yourself from two misconceptions:

1. Effective speakers are born, not made; it is hopeless to try being one if you were not gifted with a God-given ability.
2. For most people, fear and nervousness are impossible to overcome; it is useless to even try.

Let's take a look at each of these false assumptions.

Good Speakers Are Born and Not Made?

"The human brain starts working the moment you are born and never stops until you stand up to speak in public."

George Jessel

Good Speakers Are Born and Not Made?

You don't actually believe this, or you wouldn't be reading this book.

Everyone is born a baby, and babies can't speak. The "born speaker" myth is an alibi for not attempting to learn. People who believe it simply want to save face from the potential disgrace that a speech blunder may bring. They think "well, if I don't do it, I can't fail at it". WRONG! When it comes to mastering your fear of public speaking, if you don't attempt to do it, you have failed! It is a fact that practice makes perfect; you will read this throughout this book. This fear is a fear like most others; it can be overcome and mastered with practice, practice, practice!

A public speaker is one who speaks to others for a reason. When you were two or three years old and first said, "Mommy, I need a glass of water," you were making a speech. Actually you've been making speeches from the time you could talk. The difference is that you didn't treat it then as what you now dreadfully call "a speech."

You can become a good speaker if you have these tools:

1. A voice.
2. Basic language construction: i.e., a working vocabulary and grammar.
3. Something to say.
4. A need and desire to express your ideas to others.

You have been using these tools for years. You have been saying something to others, several times every day, and under these conditions, you call it "conversation." Conversation is talking to a few. Public speaking is essentially communication on a larger scale.

Your audience is merely a group of individuals. You can talk easily with one or two individuals. So just think of public speaking as talking to individuals all at the same time - or talking to the group as if they were one person.

Can You Conquer your Fear?

Here are three key solutions to help you reduce fear and make it work for you rather than against you:

1. Accept it as nature's way of helping you.

You don't need to be terrified of fear when you accept it as nature's way of protecting you and helping you. Recognize it. Don't condemn yourself for having it. We all feel fear. Whether your fear stems from the thought of standing alone by yourself on stage before hundreds of people, or even from the thought of getting on stage to speak, *keep in mind that you are responding normally*. I started where you are. I was afraid to stand and speak. But I realized that by using these tools you are now learning, developed by people who have learned to control their fear, you are winning!

Athletes are nervous before an important competition; musicians tremble before a concert; performers experience stage fright. Seasoned speakers never get rid of apprehension before speaking, nor do they want to. An experienced actor once said: "I used to have butterflies in my stomach every time I stand in front of an audience. Now that I know how to make them work for me, they fly in formation."

Knowing that you are subject to a normal and common human response, you can drive out the strongest factor contributing to your fear: *You can stop condemning yourself for being unusual.*

Psychologists tell us that fear is not the real obstacle. We feel awkward or ineffective because we think fear is improper. It is not fear itself but your feeling about it that disappoints you. Remember Franklin Roosevelt's quote: "We have nothing to fear but fear itself." As soon as you know this and recognize it, you are on your way to self-mastery.

Fear is nature's way of preparing you for danger, real or fancied. When you face a new or different circumstance, or when many are watching you and you don't want to mess up, nature does something great to help you. Recognize the help rather than being disappointed by it! Nature delivers adrenaline to your blood stream. It speeds up your pulse and your responses. It increases your blood pressure to make you more alert. It provides you with the extra energy you need for doing your best. Without the anxiety there would be no extra effort. Identify fear as a friend. Recognize it and use it well.

2. Analyze Your Fear.

Your next step in mastering fear is easy and effortless. Analyze your type of fear. Fear is a tool for protection.

What are you protecting? Are you worried about your self-esteem or what others think of you?

In public speaking there are only three dangers to self-esteem:

- Fear of yourself – fear of performing poorly or not pleasing your self-esteem.
- Fear of your audience – fear they may tease you or laugh at you.
- Fear of your material – fear you have nothing sensible to say or you are not well prepared.

Fear of yourself and fear of your audience are very much connected. It is possible to be pleasing yourself while failing to satisfy your audience. Aiming for audience approval is often a better alternative because, if you succeed, you are in fact also pleasing yourself.

But in aspiring to satisfy your audience you must never compromise your message. Sometimes you may have to give a message to people you know are particularly opposed to it. This calls for courage. Don't be afraid to incite disagreement. Good speakers have done so and have proudly walked off the stage successfully. Honest beliefs equip a speaker and give force to the speech.

Now the third, the fear of your material, the fear that you have nothing sensible to say, is also quite common. This fear is mastered by preparing your materials well in advance of your scheduled talk. By adopting the Boy Scout credo of "Be Prepared", you will almost eliminate this fear!

3. Make use of what you have learned.

You now know that fear, nature's secret weapon, can actually help you succeed. You found you were not really afraid of fear but of yourself, your audience, and your material. Now, use your knowledge. Here's how you can:

a. Hide your negative feelings from others. If you lack self-confidence, learn how to hide it. Letting the audience know about your perceived lack of self confidence won't help you in any way. Never discuss it. This will just make you feel worse. Act confidently. It will rub off on you. You will look the way you feel. Ever heard of the scared boy who walked past the cemetery one night? As long as he walked casually and whistled merrily he was all right. But when he walked faster, he could not refuse the temptation to run; and when he ran, terror took over. Don't give in to irrational fears; work to stay calm and relaxed. If it helps, pretend you are an actor, playing a role that will be seen around the world. Enjoy your talk and your audience, and use the power of visualization to help yourself.

Before each speech or presentation I do, I sit in a private and quiet area and visualize the event going smoothly- the audience smiling when I arrive on stage, the rapt attention that they have for what I am saying, and the applause at the end of my talk. I even go as far as to picture myself after the event, answering the questions I believe the audience will have, and accepting the congratulations from people in the audience.

Let me ask you something; do you think all this talk of positive visualization is ridiculous? That it is embarrassing and could not possibly work? If this is what you are thinking, then I have to tell you that you are wrong. In fact, you would be making a big mistake! Athletes, entertainers and countless others in the public eye have used positive visualization for a very long time. And they use it for one reason, because it works!

b. Assess your condition reasonably. Think of the reasons why you were called to speak. Among other possible speakers, you were chosen. Whoever asked you to speak had confidence in you, or you would not have been chosen. These people believe in you, you are thought of as a competent speaker. Consider this- if you have been asked to speak, these people believe that you know your topic, and that you know more about it than your listeners do.

Your assessment reveals that you are prepared to do well and that you have the benefit over your listeners. When you accept this, your confidence will show to your audience. It will make them believe in you and in your speech.

c. Assess your audience reasonably. They want you to do well. Listeners suffer along with a speaker who is having difficulty delivering, and they do not enjoy suffering. They would much rather react and engage you in the topic-that would give them satisfaction. So consider your audience rather than yourself. Win their interest, they will respond in kind, and as a result you will be more confident, and everybody will be happy.

Another way of putting this: Focus on a good message and speech delivery. You will make the audience happy with this and you will succeed in your mission. Do the first well, and the second will follow.

d. Assess your material reasonably. Fear of speech material is the easiest to conquer since the solution is simple: knowledge and preparation. Knowledge and preparation dispel fear, but by themselves they do not automatically assure the delivery of a successful speech.

A good start is when you recognize you don't need to be afraid – of yourself, your audience, or your material. And as you succeed in making speeches, you will soon say, "I *can* do it because I *have* done it often."

"Courage is not limited to the battlefield or the Indianapolis 500 or bravely catching a thief in your house. The real tests of courage are much quieter. They are the inner tests, like remaining faithful when nobody's looking, like enduring pain when the room is empty, like standing alone when you're misunderstood."

Charles Swindol

PART TWO

PREPARING YOUR

SPEECH

6

Nine Basic Steps in Preparing Your Speech

1. Select your topic.
2. Determine your exact purpose.
3. Identify your speech objectives.
4. Analyze your audience.
5. Plan and organize your main ideas.
6. Organize your introduction and conclusion.
7. Prepare an outline.
8. Prepare your visual aids effectively.
9. Practice your speech.

"There are always three speeches, for every one you actually gave. The one you practiced, the one you gave, and the one you wish you gave."

Dale Carnegie

Selecting Your Topic

"Grasp the subject, the words will follow."
Cato The Elder

In some instances, speakers are given a specific topic. This is most common in debating clubs or public speaking competitions. But typically you will be given an opportunity to speak with the choice of a specific topic left up to you. Once you have identified what type of speech you will be making, follow these guidelines in choosing a specific topic:

- **Choose a topic you already know a lot about.** Let's face it, when you know and enjoy the topic you are to speak on, you will feel much more relaxed and confident talking about it. So choose something you can speak with knowledge or authority about, instead of browsing the Reader's Digest and selecting a topic that you know nothing about. This is very important, and I have stressed it throughout this book, but I'll say it again... KNOW YOUR TOPIC!

- **Choose a topic you are interested in discussing.** You may know a good amount about many topics but you may not be very interested in them, so avoid these topics. It is hard to interest the audience in a subject matter that doesn't interest you. When you are excited by what you are speaking about, it shows!

- **Choose a topic that you can make interesting and/or beneficial to your listeners.** Your audience doesn't necessarily have to be interested in your topic before you speak but they absolutely must be when you are finished speaking. If you analyze your potential listeners, you must have a strong understanding of their interests. This goes back to the previous point; if you possess an interest in what you are speaking about, it shows. And consider this; if you possess a strong knowledge of the topics that interest your audience, your success in communicating effectively with them is virtually assured.

- **Choose a topic that suits the requirements of the assignment.** Be sure you know the type of speech, the time constraints, and any other requirements, and choose your topic accordingly. This requires you to plan and rehearse your speech; check your timing (I use a digital timer), and video yourself at least twice to see how you are performing in your presentation.

You may also want to conduct a self-inventory to help you come up with possible topics. Ask yourself the following:

- What are my intellectual and educational interests?

- What do I like to read?
- What interesting things have I learned from newspapers?
- What interesting things have I learned from television?
- What particular courses, or topics covered in courses, have specifically interested me?
- What are my career goals? What do I hope to do in my life?
- What are my favorite leisure activities and interests?
- What things do I do for fun that others might like to learn more about or take part in?
- What personal and social concerns are significant to me?
- What is going on in my life that bothers or affects me?
- What is happening outside my immediate world that is unfair, unjust, or in need of improvement?

Narrowing Down the Topic

Once you have chosen your general topic, you are ready to narrow it down on the basis of your listener's interests and needs. Here are the steps to follow in narrowing down a topic:

1. **Choose potential speech topics (from self-inventory).**

2. **Consider situational factors.**

   - *Familiarity*: Will my listeners be familiar with any information that will help me select a topic?

   - *Current events*: Can I select a topic to emphasize current events that may be of significant interest to my audience?

   - *Audience apathy*: Can I encourage my audience to be actively interested toward topics that are totally relevant to me?

   - *Time limits*: Do I have enough time to discuss the topic sufficiently?

3. **Consider audience factors.**

   - *Previous knowledge*: Very important! What do my listeners already know about my topic?

   - *Common experiences*: What common experiences have my listeners encountered?

   - *Common interests*: Where do my interests and my listeners' meet?

   - *Relevant diverse factors*: How diverse are the backgrounds of my listeners.

4. **Select your tentative topic.**

Some examples of narrowing down may be seen on the next page:

GENERAL TOPIC	NARROWED DOWN	NARROWED DOWN FURTHER	NARROWED DOWN EVEN FURTHER
Career Choices	career choices of graduates of top American schools	career choices of graduates of top American schools in the last 5 years	factors affecting the career choices of MBA graduates of Wharton School of Business in the last 5 years
Southeast Asia	security problems in Southeast Asia	roots of terrorism in Southeast Asia	cooperation among governments of Southeast Asia in addressing the problems of terrorism
Housing	housing projects in the last 10 years	housing projects in City X	financing problems in the housing projects in City X

Determining Your Exact Purpose

Begin with the end in mind. I see one thing in common with virtually every beginner that I coach, and that is they start by thinking about what they want to say. Experienced speakers begin by deciding exactly what they want the outcome of their speech to be. The basic purposes of public speaking are to inform, to instruct, to entertain, and to persuade. These four are not mutually exclusive of one another. A speaker may have several purposes in mind. It may be to inform and also to entertain. Another speaker may want to inform and at the same time convince, stimulate, or persuade. Although content, organization, and delivery may have two or more purposes, most have just one central purpose.

Speeches that *inform* offer accurate data, objective information, findings, and on occasions, interpretations of these findings. Those that *instruct* teach the audience a process or a procedure based on information provided in the speech. Those that *entertain* provide pleasure and enjoyment that make the audience laugh or identify with delightful situations.

Finally, speeches that *persuade* try to convince the audience to take a certain stand on an issue, an idea, or a belief, by appealing first to reason through logical arguments and evidence, and to the emotions by crafting statements that will move your audience.

Identifying the Objectives of the Speech

An objective is more limited and specific than a purpose. It may target behavior or thought. What does the message communicated in the speech expect to accomplish? What response does it invite from the audience? Does it want to convince the listeners to support a cause by joining a movement? Does it want the listeners to buy a certain product or use a certain service? Does it want the listeners to modify their behavior through a process presented? Does it want to move the listeners to laughter and later to reflection about a significant social issue? Does it want to provide accurate and credible information to lead them to a decision? As answers to these questions are given, speech objectives can be identified and stated.

Here are some examples:

Topic	Purpose	Objectives
A Call for Support for independence in Old Age	to persuade	The speech will seek pledges of effort, time, or money to help establish an institution to support independency in old age.
Why My Goal in Life Is to Become a Lawyer	to inform	After hearing my speech, the audience will understand why my dream is to become a lawyer.

7

Analyzing Your Audience

"They may forget what you said, but they will never forget how you made them feel."

Carl W. Buechner

Remember the old saying, walk a mile in my shoes? Well this is certainly relevant to public speaking!

The more you know about your audience, the better you will be able to connect your topic to them. Audience analysis is not difficult. It basically requires knowing your audience so that you can organize your verbal, visual, and vocal delivery to suit the situation and their expectations. When analyzing an audience, you aren't trying to deceive, control, or force them; you are just making sure your speech suits them and keeps them interested. Try to look at things form the audience's point of view, and you will greatly increase the attention paid to you by your audience.

Speeches need to be audience-centered; so audience analysis is a must. For example, if you are speaking to an audience who has been compelled to attend your presentation (sales meeting, training seminar), you need to tell them at the beginning specifically how they will benefit from what you are talking about. Be aware; if you are making a business presentation you must recognize that there could be members of the audience with a hidden agenda- that is to say that they may attempt to discredit your ideas or disrupt your presentation in some way. Of course it would be nearly impossible to foresee all potential hazards in a situation like this, but by being aware, you can be more prepared. Remember the old saying, "fore warned is fore armed".

Design presentation – content, organization, and delivery – is influenced by the kind of audience expected at the presentation so make sure they understand the meaning and significance of the message. For effectiveness, a speaker should know the following:

1. Who are the listeners?

Try to take note of the general age, range, male-female ratio, educational background, occupation or profession, ethnic background, religion, geographical or cultural environment, civic status, income level and assets, group and organizational memberships, etc. of your audience. By being aware of these factors, you can make the appropriate adjustments to your presentation, in a way tailoring it more to your audience and its needs.

What do they want from you?

Are they there to receive instructions? Do they want current issues explained? Do they also want to have fun? Do they need information? Have they come on their own or were they required to attend? Voluntary audiences are likely to be homogeneous; this means of same kind: having the same kind of constituent elements, or being similar in nature, in other words, they have things in common; they *want* to be there. Classroom students make up an involuntary audience; they are heterogeneous; which is defined as consisting of dissimilar parts: consisting of parts or aspects that are unrelated or unlike each other, in other words, they vary in many ways, and, you guessed it, they would probably rather be anywhere else but listening to you!

3. What is the size of the audience?

How large is the audience? Is it an audience of 20 or 200? In a classroom, you would be speaking to around thirty students. But in other settings, you may be speaking to a smaller group (like a buzz group) or a bigger group (like a rally).

Audience size may add to anxiety and may affect speech delivery, more so in the use of visual aids, the type of language you use, and so on. Overall, you want to speak more formally with larger groups. You also need to be very aware of your strength of delivery and the tonality of your voice. In a classroom setting, you will be speaking about 20% louder than conversational level to be heard. Now if you are speaking in a lecture hall, arena, or other large area, you must adjust your voice and timing of delivery appropriately. Imagine this; you are standing at the edge of a canyon, and you yell "hello……" what comes back to you? Your voice of course, repeated several times courtesy of the echo. Well the echo effect exists in arenas and other large spaces as well.

You may think that because you have a microphone, the people in the back of the room can hear you just fine, but be aware that echo, noise from the audience, and poor vocalization can cause parts of your audience to miss what you are trying to say. Probably not what you had in mind! I strongly encourage you to seek out audio or video presentations of speakers such as Martin Luther King, John F. Kennedy, and Billy Graham. These are men who understood the value of measured delivery in their presentations. By this I mean that they had a clear understanding of the place they were speaking, were aware of the echo and crowd noise, and they adjusted the way they delivered their speeches accordingly.

4. Where is the venue of the presentation?

Will the venue be a room? What kind of room will it be - a conference room, a hall perhaps, or a small meeting room?

When you speak in a classroom, you are speaking in a familiar, comfortable setting. You know whether there is an overhead projector, whether the lights can be dimmed, and so on.

As you do speeches, you will learn more about other settings for public speaking, like outdoor stages, or malls and even hotel conference rooms. You may be curious to know how it feels speaking while standing at floor level versus standing in a stage. It is very important for you to learn about podiums, technological support, microphones, the sound system, and so on. One of the worst things that can occur to shake your confidence is to step up to the podium and begin speaking…..into a dead microphone! I make a special point of meeting the technical support people and having them familiarize me with the equipment prior to my presentation. These people are also very helpful in showing you the best way to light your speaking area, and giving you tips on the best way to move through the room and maintain visual and audio connection with your audience.

Audience analysis can and should be done before the presentation, though most times you need to make adjustments during the presentation itself. A sensitive speaker receives a great deal of information from listeners as the talk is being given. Often, the cues are nonverbal, such as attentiveness, facial expressions, restlessness, passiveness, or apathy. When these signs show, you need to be flexible enough to adjust or modify to do a better job of delivering your presentation. Shifting places, gestures, voice changes, or maybe even audience involvement can prove to be useful. Be resourceful!

Here's an example of audience analysis:

Topic: A Call for Support for an aging population in your area

Purpose: To Persuade

Objective/s: The speech will seek pledges of effort, time, or money to help establish an institution to support and enhance the lives of older citizens in the community.

Audience Analysis:

1. Who are the listeners?	• Heads/officers of civic, religious and business communities in the city • Almost equal ratio of men and women who are professionals, with high educational attainments and high earning capacity, leaders in their specific fields, dominantly Christian audience with 65% Catholics, 85% married, American and American-Chinese, some south Asians • Active in social and civic works • In touch with current political, social, and religious issues • In touch with prevailing business and government situations
2. What do they want from you?	• Basically interested in a topic that is relevant to their group or organization • Desire to get more information about dependency of old age, and to know more about what the speaker is going to propose/request • Want enough information to decide whether or not to support the cause you are addressing
3. What is the size of the audience?	• 50 people
4. Where is the venue of the presentation?	• Medium-sized case room with fixed upholstered seats in a semi-circle • 2-ft elevation in the front for the speaker • Very good acoustics • Electronic devices for presentations

So, by completing an analysis like this each time you are going to do a presentation, you gain a much better understanding of what is required to make your presentation successful.

Visit my website at **www.speakandwin.com** to download a free audience analysis checklist. Remember Ben Franklin's immortal words; "By failing to prepare, you are preparing to fail". Take the time to complete this important analysis each time and be prepared!

PART THREE

DEVELOPING YOUR SPEECH

8

Organizing Your Speech

"It takes one hour of preparation for each minute of presentation time."

Wayne Burgraff

A lot of speakers cautiously choose their topics, select a concrete purpose, look for good supporting resources, and yet never experience success in public speaking. It may be partly due to misfortune, but it can be mostly attributed to how they have outlined and organized their thoughts.

It is like writing an essay. You need to start with a thesis and decide the main points that will clarify or develop it. Organizing, therefore, is stating the thesis of the speech and listing down the main ideas that will be used to support it.

THE REMEMBER BOX

Organizing the presentation has three parts: the introduction, body, and conclusion. It is a thesis developed with support points. Discourse markers and transition devices tie the parts together.

Organizing the Introduction of Your Speech

The beginning of your speech is critical. It gives your audience their first impression of your subject, purpose, and main point. But your beginning must do more than help them to understand your speech. It must also catch their interest. It is not sufficient to say, "Today I am going to talk about why the school needs a new basketball gym." It's difficult to captivate the audience using this statement. The introduction needs to be planned so that listeners want to pay attention to your speech, consider you as a credible speaker, and have some notion of your speech's focus and objective. The better opening is "a new basketball gym will help our children and our school prosper, and I'm going to tell you how this can be done quickly".

Some other examples:

Bad: Today I will talk about the relevance of form 21b in your expense filings

Good: I have some vital information to share with you that will show you how to get your expense check quicker than before, and help eliminate wasted time!

Bad: I want to tell you that there are 8 things from various departments that we need to address today, so please pay attention.

Good: We have 8 issues on the agenda today that have an impact on each of our jobs, so let's discuss what they are, and get some results!

Can you see the differences in these good and bad openings? The good ones have a common thread in them; they are brief, to the point, speak of a benefit to the listener, and have some enthusiasm. I live by the line Elvis said in that famous song, "little less conversation, a little more action, please"!

A lot of good speeches fall short because of their confusing and boring introductions. If you do not get off to a good start then chances are your audience may "tune you out," like a radio listener who simply changes channels to get rid of silly programs. Just because people sit as part of the audience does not mean they intend to listen – it is your job to make it impossible for them not to.

Effective introduction includes capturing the attention of your audience. When you get up to speak, the audience will usually give you their full attention. But that attention is short. Below are ways of maintaining audience attention:

- ***Establish common ground.*** Listeners are more likely to pay attention to speakers with whom they share common experiences, problems, or goals. You have seen this many times in your life, but may not have been particularly aware of it.

Consider Martin Luther King Jr. and his speeches; he sought first to establish a common thread between the positions that he was going to make, and then he began to draw the audience to him by painting word pictures that the audience could immerse themselves in. Just remembering the words he spoke, "I have a dream" still sends shivers through me. This is the art of creating the common ground. Sit back in your chair for a minute, close your eyes, and hear the words of your favorite speech; I'd be willing to bet you can visualize the speaker, feel the passion in their voice. This is what defines OK speakers from great speakers. They build the foundation that links them to their audience.

- ***A startling statement or statistic.*** Use intriguing or startling statements or statistics that arouse curiosity. For example, "950,000 people in the Middle East may not be able to eat three meals a day in the year 2012." or "Dinosaurs aren't extinct. Every time you see a songbird, you're looking at a survivor from the Paleozoic era." This gets people's attention. Now you need to be careful with this, because you can easily be seen as the carnival barker, trying to get people into the circus tent. You don't want people to be disappointed when they realize that your statement has very little to do with the speech you are giving. But hey, presented well these statements make people sit up and pay attention, and at the end of the day, that is why you are there talking to them!

- *A story or a brief anecdote.* An interesting story – whether it is emotional, humorous, puzzling, or intriguing – commands attention. The story can be factual or fancied. It can be a personal experience, or it can be something you have read. For example, "An interesting thing happened on my way here today." or "The first time I jumped out of a plane...". Standup comedy has its roots in the "story". The classic opening lines like "a funny thing happened on the way here" and "So this woman says to me..." are all the beginning of what the final joke will be. By taking a lesson from this approach, and leading the audience into the story in this fashion, the speaker has now captured their attention, and they are more likely to keep the audience engaged throughout the speech or presentation.

- **A rhetorical or actual question.** Rhetorical questions don't ask for immediate responses. Instead, they are aimed to get the audience thinking about an issue or concept. For example, "Did you know that you lose ten billion skin cells every day?" or "how do you intend to save the planet for the next generation?". Again, you want the question to be provocative and thought inducing, all the while positioning the audience to engage in your speech or presentation.

- **A quotation.** You can use the words of a famous performer, author, athlete, or singer or other renowned and highly esteemed figures to get the audience's interest and attention immediately. For example, "When I was a small child, I heard a wise man say….". You have no doubt noticed that I frequently use quotes in this book; I do this for several reasons, two of which are that I deeply value the thoughts of certain people who have passed through the history of mankind. Secondly, I believe that there is much to be learned from these words. I have encountered quotes from people who have passed from sight and earthly existence sometimes thousands of years ago, and yet I find their words inspiring and thought provoking even today. Choose your quotes carefully, and be prepared to illustrate how they bear relevance to what you are speaking about.

- **_Use humor._** Some speakers love to start a speech with a humorous anecdote, but you have to handle humor with care. Regardless of how funny a story is, it must be appropriate to the point you want to make. Merely telling a few jokes is not a good way to introduce a speech, and a joke that falls flat is humiliating. Humor should never be rude and should never be intended to ridicule someone or something, so you have to be cautious.

You can use several of the above simultaneously. For instance, you might tell an interesting story that also establishes common ground and piques curiosity.

Pausing after telling a compelling story, asking a rhetorical question, or sharing a memorable quotation may help audience members reflect on and remember what you are about to say. In whatever technique you use, be sure it attracts in the sense that a magnet attracts. The important factor here is capturing and maintaining the listeners' interest and attention. These are commonly called anchors.

Now generally speaking, people do not control or create their anchors or links consciously. They just happen! Your mind makes them without you knowing! But what if you could create and use the same method that your mind does to help people focus on what you want them to remember from your presentation?

Well that would be an INCREDIBLE tool for you to use to shape, mould, and control your message. Imagine for a second, how would you like to be able to instantly get your audience into an energetic and mentally focused state?

I'm sure you are all saying to yourself right now "That would be GREAT!"

An effective introduction gets attention and generates audience interest on the topic. It also creates appropriate expectations by preparing the listeners to receive the message. What three distinct parts make up the introduction?

1. **The opener** – This is the first sentence. It can be a quotation, a startling statement or statistic, or a brief anecdote. This opening should be short, interesting, and appropriate to the topic.
2. **The topic** – This is simply stating the title of the speech. Say it directly as: "I have been asked to speak about _____." or

"I have chosen to speak to you about
_____."

3. **The agenda** – This briefly explains your points of view or what you will be discussing.

Here then is an example of an introduction:

Good afternoon, everyone. It's a pleasure to be here with you today. I have been asked to introduce myself and been given 3 minutes to do this. There is not much I can tell you about myself in that length of time; so, what I will do instead is to start with my topic which is *The increasing involvement of concerned citizens in environmental issues today*. I feel very strongly that the responses to current social issues are evident in one, the increased interest in the urban environment and two, citizen participation or support of community-based groups for change, and three, increased involvement in national issues through a stronger sense of awareness of these issues.

These sentences are the **openers**, the **topic** and the **agenda**.

In effect, the introduction is brief, direct, and should get the audience's attention while preparing them for what is to follow. In an interesting manner, an introduction clearly establishes the topic and sets a guide on what the audience can expect from the speech.

Organizing the Body of Your Speech

At this point you're set to organize your main ideas and provide visual and verbal supports. The body of your speech is its meat, and you should put the major points you want to expound in this portion of your speech. These main points must be simple, declarative sentences so that they are easily recognized and remembered when people leave your speech. These points need support, elaboration, clarification, and evidence. These can come in the form of specific and concrete details, comparisons, examples, and illustrations. Remember too that you are going to reiterate these points at the end of your speech, in the summary.

There are several steps you can do to make your main points memorable:

1. Limit yourself to no more than three to five main points. Any more than this will confuse your audience.
2. Keep your main points brief and use parallel structures when possible. Parallel structure means using the same pattern of words to show that two or more ideas have the same level of importance.
3. Arrange your material so that you cover your most important point either first or last.

4. Make your main points memorable by creating your own rhyme or acronym when possible. For example, here is a typical sales acronym; SMART=Specific, Measurable, Achievable, Realistic, Timely. I like acronyms because they can stick in people's minds, sometimes long after the talk is over.

Organizing the Conclusion of Your Speech

A common shortcoming of many speakers is that they don't actually conclude their speeches – they merely stop talking. Others may fall through their concluding paragraph, decreasing the success of the speech.

The concluding paragraph is very essential. It gradually ushers the audience back to an overall assessment of the discussion. Of course, a competent discussion in the body will give the speaker more leeway to devise a conclusion to this effect.

No speech is complete without a concluding remark since the conclusion ensures all ideas were understood and remembered. It provides the needed closure. It's very likely that some might have missed, have misunderstood, or have forgotten a point (perhaps they were unfocused or they were daydreaming for a while). Without a conclusion, we cannot correct these problems. A conclusion is essential because listeners like and need closure. Without it, they may feel like vacationers left adrift after a pleasure cruise – much of the enjoyment created by the cruise is lost.

The conclusion is particularly significant if you have a question-and-answer period at the last part of your speech. Provide a brief summary before the question-and-answer and another one after it to tie up any loose ends and to redirect attention back to the main points presented in your speech.

But like the beginning, the ending should be relatively brief, preferably not more than one-seventh of the whole speech. Most devices suggested for beginnings are appropriate for endings. The shorter you make your ending, the more forceful it will seem to your audience, and the more easily they will remember it.

Here are some techniques to create effective conclusions:

1. Summarize what you have told your audience – your main points and ideas. "So, in summary..."
2. Issue a challenge to your audience. "Will you step up and help control the citizen's tax burden in our city?"

3. Make an appeal to your audience for action. "We need your help to succeed"

4. Visualize the future. "Imagine the world your children will experience"

5. Include memorable quotations. "As Franklin D. Roosevelt said, Only thing we have to fear, is fear itself"

6. Refer to the introduction, i.e. return the audience to your opening statement. "When I began, I told you I would show you how we can reduce Civic debt by 10%, and I believe I have illustrated that to you tonight."

Since conclusions are so essential and potentially memorable, they should (1) be brief, (2) never ramble, (3) not introduce new information, and (4) be constructed carefully. As you can see, the conclusion of a speech is too crucial to take lightly. If you make your conclusion carefully, then you will end your speech with a strategic close and produce a final positive effect.

If you see that time is running out, don't remove your conclusion. It is better to shorten your final point than to exclude your conclusion. But remember, if you time your speech while practicing, you won't have to be bothered about any time problems.

The time to conclude is when the audience wants more and not when the speaker has exhausted them. A proper and well constructed conclusion helps your audience to absorb and retain all information and your central message and you make it easy for them to follow the logical steps you have spoken to them about.

> "Make sure you have finished speaking before your audience has finished listening."
> **Dorothy Sarnoff**

9

OUTLINING YOUR SPEECH

What is your reaction the moment you hear the word outline? If your instant reaction is a negative one, perhaps you have never actually learned how to outline properly, or maybe your previous experiences with writing have recalled less-than-fond memories. Whatever the reason, you are not alone – a lot of people hate outlining. This hatred is unfortunate, because when applied properly, outlines can save you considerable time and can help you develop a much higher quality speech. Your outline might just a list of topics, or it might be a formal document itself. It depends on what you are planning to speak about and how much detail you need in your speech. Proper composition of an outline is critical to your success in delivering a speech or presentation, because it is the foundation of it.

Basic Principles of Outlining

Outlining will not only help you see the general idea of your speech. It will also help you subdivide the body of your message into sub-topics according to the order of their significance. Outlining always helps - sometimes a little, sometimes a lot – but it always helps.

What Is an Outline?

    A. An outline is a system of note-taking that shows how somebody has organized a group of ideas.

    B. It also shows how these ideas are related to one another.

Steps To Follow When Outlining

    C. Try to discover the most important idea or the main idea.

        1. You should write this as a title or thesis statement.

        2. Think in exact terms when outlining.

    D. Look for major ways to develop or subdivide the main point. (This will provide you with the major headings of your outline.) Consider signals or transition words to indicate:

        1. Chronological order

        2. Enumeration

        3. Cause-effect relationships

        4. General to specific/easy to difficult

        5. Comparison-contrast

    E. Try to stress details.

        1. Stress what you think is important or complicated and in need of more detailed explanation.

2. Always try to connect these details to the major points.

Notation In Outlining

F. The size of the indentation and the notation used are determined by the importance of the idea.

1. The most important or primary ideas are placed to the farthest left and are noted with roman numerals (I, II, III, etc.).

2. The next most important ideas (the major details) are placed below the primary ideas and are noted with capital letters (A, B, C, etc.).

3. The minor details are placed to the right below the major details and are noted with plain numbers (1, 2, 3, etc.).

G. All ideas of the same importance should have equal indention, with all major or main ideas being assigned with roman numerals and being farthest to the left.

H. You may write items in an outline as either phrases or sentences, but the entire outline should be one or the other. In other words, don't mix phrases and sentences in the same outline.

I. Always capitalize the first word of each item in an outline.

J. Always place a period after each notation symbol (numbers and letters) in an outline.

What are the Advantages of Outlining?

K. It is easier to identify problems.

L. It is less difficult to ask for sensible evaluations.

M. There is less temptation to memorize your speech.

N. Flexibility is increased.

Outlining can be a time-consuming experience but the process is well worth the effort you put into it. Once you practice and get comfortable with your own outlining process, I think that you will see that it is one of the best ways to guarantee organized writing sessions, and your efforts will result in a well-structured, effective framework for your presentation.

PART FOUR

PRESENTING YOUR SPEECH

10

Preparing Your Visual Aids Effectively

I am sure that you have heard the saying "a picture is worth a thousand words"? You know, when it comes to creating dynamic presentations this statement could not be more true! One of the easiest methods to guarantee a successful and effective speech is to use interesting and powerful visual aids. Unfortunately, a lot of speakers either don't use visual aids at all or use overcrowded, difficult-to-read visuals that make it almost impossible for the audience to understand the visuals' content, to listen to the talk, and to take down notes all together.

Poorly designed visual aids compel listeners to decide between listening to the speaker or reading the visual aid – and typically they choose to tune you out and read. Thus when preparing your visuals remember that if listeners will take much longer than seven seconds to grasp the content, they will likely fall into a reading mode. Most people take more information in visually, even when they are reading something because it is processed and stored as a visual thought or picture in our minds. When listeners are thrown into a reading mode, they hear almost nothing the speaker says.

Audiovisual aids should only be used to reinforce, explain, or further clarify the main points of a presentation; they are not intended to be the presentation. By my experience, even excellent visuals will not save a weak presentation. Audiovisual aids range from simple flipcharts or graphs, to PowerPoint or DVD. Communication effectiveness is frequently enhanced by the use of more than one medium.

Functions of Visual Aids

Visual aids, when used effectively, can help a speaker communicate better and can help listeners understand better. Visual aids engage the senses (what we see and what we hear) and help clarify, support, and strengthen the message. Visual aids are so effective that most speakers use them. The use of visual aids will move you further along toward your objectives by illustrating and emphasizing your ideas more effectively than words alone.

Visual aids help you reach your objectives by providing emphasis to whatever is being said. Clear pictures multiply the audience's level of understanding of the material presented, and they should be used to reinforce your message to your audience, provide clarifying points, and create an exciting presentation for your audience.

As I mentioned earlier, visual aids completely involve your audience and therefore require a change from one activity to another: from listening to seeing. When you use visual aids, it usually requires gestures and movement on your part. This extra movement reinforces the control that you, the speaker, have over the flow and direction of the presentation. Most importantly, visual aids add impact and interest to a presentation. They will enable you to appeal to more than one sense at the same time, thereby increasing the audience's understanding and retention level.

A majority of people tend to rely on seeing (visual), rather than hearing (auditory), hence the need for presentations that combine speech (words), and pictures (visual). Again, I stress the impact that properly designed visual aids bring to a presentation can be significant indeed. The studies below reveal interesting statistics that support these findings:

- In many studies that I have conducted or researched, I have found that retention of information three days after a meeting or other event is six times greater when information is presented by visual and oral means than when the information is presented by the spoken word alone.

- Research suggests that approximately 83% of human learning occurs visually (by seeing words or graphs), and the remaining 17% through the other senses - 11% through hearing, 3.5% through smell, 1% through taste, and 1.5% through touch.
- Research indicates that three days after an event, people retain 10% of what they heard from an oral presentation, 35% from a visual presentation, and 65% from a visual and oral presentation.

In summary, let's consider the ways in which visual aids can improve your presentation. Visual aids can:

- provide support and emphasize main ideas
- facilitate understanding
- encourage emotional involvement
- aid with delivery
- add to your credibility
- Decrease your nervousness because they give you something to do with your hands, they can draw audience attention away from you, and they make it almost impossible to forget what you want to say.

Listeners also benefit from the effective use of visual aids. Such aids can:

- help separate important from less important information
- add interest and color
- improve audience retention of your presentation

PowerPoint

We are all aware that blackboards, White boards, flip charts and overheads are useful, but in today's multi-media world, PowerPoint is the king, so let's get right to it!

Steven's top 10 steps to Creating Awesome Powerpoint Presentations:

1. **Choose the correct background or template.**The proper template is an important choice. You want to use templates that are in color focus with your presentation. For example, a wild and colourful background is not going to win friends at the brokerage firm. Choose backgrounds that fit the tone of your presentation.

2. **Choose font colors carefully.** Color can highlight or distract. Just like I stated in point 1, make sure that

the font color fits the tone you are trying to set with your presentation.

3. **AVOID UPPER CASE.** As you can see, it's just too much. The presentation should read just like it was on a page.

4. **Avoid the !?.** It's easy to fall into the trap of using too many exclamation and question marks. You might feel that the liberal use of them highlights your point, but it does not. The key is to let your voice make the point as you are working through your PowerPoint presentation.

5. **Make good use of charts and graphs.** Recall I have said in this book that people absorb much more information when they see *and* hear it. But caution: make sure that your charts and graphs are relevant to your presentation, and don't overdo it!

6. **Create graphics that enhance your text.** Just as with the charts and graphs be careful. You do not want to let the graphics take away from your verbal message.

7. **State your message as the title of each slide.** Then develop the message visually in the body of each slide, this helps re-enforce your message.

8. **Use animation sparingly.** I don't favour using any animation, as I feel that it can too easily destract the audience from the message.

9.   **Use hyperlinks carefully.** As with animation they can be a distraction. In the age of the iphone it's rather easy for the audience to go to the link during your presentation. Very distracting for the audience and you when you see heads looking down. If you must use them, give them as a separate take home sheet for the audience.

10.   **Back up-or else.** Can't stress this one enough, because I have deleted hours of work in the errant press of a key. Back up every 60 seconds. You'll thank me later!

"Power corrupts; PowerPoint corrupts absoloutely"

Edward Tufte

11

DELIVERING YOUR MESSAGE EFFECTIVELY

"I do not object to people looking at their watches when I am speaking, but I strongly object when they start shaking them to make sure they are still working"

Lord Birkett

When I began taking a serious interest in developing my skills as a speaker and presenter, one of my mentors strongly advised me to invest in a video camera to record myself as I practiced my presentations, and to record myself while I was delivering a presentation.

Recording a presentation while you practice delivers two important benefits to you; first, you will be able to watch your practice run and see where your weak spots are. Now you can note them, correct them and then record yourself again. Keep doing this until you are satisfied with your presentation. Now after you record yourself actually presenting the speech in front of an audience, you can go back, watch both the practice and the final presentation, and compare the two side by side. This is a critical step in developing your skills, and can save you a huge amount of time, as it will help you identify and correct any weaknesses you have. I cannot recommend this step to you strongly enough; it was a huge aid in my own development.

After all the preparations that go into your speech, you eventually present yourself to the audience. You may have spent days or even weeks to analyze your potential listeners, select your topic, organize and rehearse your speech, but you will finish your speech delivery in just a matter of minutes. Nevertheless, the actual delivery is the highlight and finale of the public speaking experience.

If one were to ask a listener what he thought of a speech that had just been delivered, the reply would be something like: "I think she has a very pleasant voice, or I think he should have moved around more, or "I couldn't always hear her."

Obviously, delivery is not everything in public speaking. A good delivery cannot compensate for a poorly prepared message, or one lacking in substance. Despite that, most of us know the significance of delivery, and at times it scares us. We may feel at ease preparing the speech, conducting the research, organizing and outlining our ideas, and so on. However, when faced with the actual "standing and delivering," we may become very nervous.

The more we know about delivery, the better our chances of doing it successfully. Delivery may not be everything in speech development, but it is obviously an important part.

Take for instance, the case of a famous talk-show host - Oprah Winfrey. As of the writing of this book, Oprah's show is coming to an end after 25 years on the air. Her show consistently lead in the talk-show ratings. How does she do it? She is enthusiastic, interesting, powerful, persuasive, caring, and – most important of all – believable. She appears as if she is speaking directly to each member of her audience-she is real, and she is believable. She does more than just organize convincing ideas; she presents her thoughts in a believable way. She knows how to connect with her audience by communicating with them verbally, visually, and vocally. And so can you.

Your delivery isn't more essential than what you have to say, but without good delivery your listeners may never hear what you have to say. To make your presentation believable, you must practice.

Visual Delivery

Because the first impression comes more from what the audience see than from what they hear, we will first talk about visual delivery – particularly, how to appear to your audience. As a public speaker, your physical appearance, posture, facial expressions, eye contact, body movements, and gestures all influence your audience's perception.

The audience judges your **appearance** as a hint to your position, credibility, and knowledge. Unless you are sure about what is suitable for the audience and the occasion, the safest thing to do is to dress conservatively.

Good posture is nothing more than standing straight and having your "chest out" and "stomach in." Proper posture makes the speaker look and feel comfortable, and aids voice projection and poise.

MOVE IT! **Body movement** can add interest, energy, and confidence to your presentation. Don't be pacing back and forth on the stage, and try to avoid standing too far back on the stage; it makes it difficult for those seated close to the stage to see you. When I do presentations, I work the front 6 feet of the stage. This makes it easy for people in the audience to see me, and easier for me to make eye contact with the audience, which is critical in delivering an effective presentation. To add emphasis, try moving at the beginning of an idea or at a transition between ideas.

Gestures are movements of the hands, arms, head, and the shoulders to help you communicate. They play an important role in public speaking, but they must enhance communication and not hinder it. Try making the gestures when rehearsing a speech. Practice before a mirror, even to the point of exaggerating. Then adapt your gestures to a point where they are appropriate and natural. Remember, gestures should be spontaneous. Too many gestures may distract the audience and make you look nervous and poorly prepared.

One kind of gesture is **facial expression**. This reveals your attitudes and feelings. Let your face glow with happiness or burn with enthusiasm. Avoid wearing the deadpan poker face that reveals nothing. This doesn't mean that you will always give vent to your feelings in an extravagant manner. A good speaker expresses views and feelings with appropriate restraint. And consider this; you may think that people in the far reaches of the room can't see your face, but you are wrong. When you are on a properly lit stage, you are very visible to all in the room!

Eye contact is a very important factor in getting and holding attention. Look at your listeners directly, not above them or at the floor or ceiling or out of the window; otherwise, you lose your contact with your audience and their attention strays off. My simple rule on eye contact is this: keep looking for someone to be making contact with. A good strategy for eye contact is to make brief eye contact with members of the audience in one section of the audience, and then as you move around the stage move your eye contact to new people. Ideally, you should be making eye contact with someone whenever you are speaking. Now beware of falling into this trap; people will naturally tend to focus their eye contact on the person that is giving them the best nonverbal feedback such as smiling and nodding. It is important to make eye contact for a few seconds, and then to move on to others. Share the attention!

Here are some questions you might consider in order to guide your visual delivery:

- Do I gesture enough? Too much?
- Does my body movement reinforce the flow of my speech?
- Are my gestures disturbing in any way?
- Am I depending too much on any one gesture?
- Does my face express the meaning or feeling I am trying to convey?
- Are there different gestures, body movements, or facial expressions that might express my intended meaning more effectively?

Vocal Delivery

We all like to have an effective, pleasant voice. Voice is essential in communication-it is only through voice that any speech delivery be accomplished.

An effective voice is conversational, natural, and enthusiastic. It is pleasant to hear without having to be forced or strained. The audience will listen more if you speak as you do in a normal conversation.

Sounds have four fundamental characteristics: volume, pitch, rate, and quality. If any of these is faulty, distraction results. Important announcements are uttered in a slow manner and with a relatively low pitch, whereas jokes or other light remarks are uttered in a rapid fashion with a relatively higher pitch. For some good practice, watch an old Seinfeld rerun; you'll have some laughs, and you will see mastery at work. Jerry delivers lines that keep people hanging on each word, because he measures the timing and delivery of each sentence. If you wish to develop a pleasing and dynamic personality in your presentations, practice the tips on voice projection listed here. Learning these fundementals of speech will greatly enhance your self confidence!

1. Volume

A well-modulated voice is important to be an effective speaker. Many people have very soft voices, which can be due to shyness or lack of training or lack of practice in voice projection. People with soft voices are often regarded as shy or dull.

There is no hard and fast rule about the degree of loudness that should be used on different occasions, but an effective voice must be as loud as the specific speaking situation requires. If you are speaking to a group, every member of the audience with normal hearing and concentration should be able to understand your statements without straining their ears and without getting irritated because of an excessively loud voice. Good speakers fit voice and actions to the words used, to the situation, and to their personalities. An important principle in speaking clearly is that consonants should be pronounced well. Vowels are easier to pronounce, yet consonants give intelligibility to speech.

A voice that is dominated by intellect rather than emotion tends to be moderate in pitch as well as in loudness. This does not imply that intellectual efforts are devoid of feeling. It just implies that intellectual efforts accompanied by vocalization are not normally characterized by the exaggerated range and intensity of feeling exhibited in emotional behavior alone.

2. Pitch

Pitch refers to the general level on a musical scale of the voice in speech. If a person is habitually tense, the voice is often in a higher pitch level than that of a habitually relaxed person. Pitch may either be high, medium, or low; or we may use such terms as soprano, alto, baritone, or bass for vocal pitch.

Natural pitch in speaking is important for an effective voice. One who speaks unnaturally will be ineffective, disagreeable, and uncomfortable and cause strain to their voice. When you moderate your pitch according to the emphasis on the point you are trying to make in your presentation, your voice sounds natural.

3. Rate

There are three rates or tempos in speaking – slow, average, and fast. A markedly slow speaking rate indicates solemnity, sorrow, or depression. A marked increase in rate is suggestive of happiness, joy, elation, or passion. Words or phrases that are spoken more slowly and more emphatically are considered more important and more intellectually significant than rapidly pronounced words. However, a sustained, unchanging rate of speaking is discouraged regardless of feeling, mood, or purpose because it is monotonous.

Changes in rate can be achieved by the rate of articulation or by the use of pauses. The use of pauses is a very useful technique for separating or grouping phrases, for creating dramatic effects, and for emphasizing ideas. As a general rule, the use of a comma is a sign for the reader or speaker to pause. But in some instances, long sentences without commas should also be divided according to thought content by a pause to give time for breathing and for the listener to grasp fully what is being read or said.

Dramatic effect can be achieved by speakers who pause after a rising inflection, thereby creating suspense, after which the expected outcome follows to the satisfaction of their listeners.

4. Quality

Voice characteristics and voice attitudes come under the general term of voice quality. A person's voice can be categorized as pleasant or unpleasant depending upon its timbre and / or quality. What is voice quality? This term is hard to identify and no attempt will be made to define it here except to show its relations to other factors and how to achieve this. Vocal quality is related to resonance and to the avoidance of undesirable vocal aspects such as excessive nasality and breathing. It is also related to feeling and mood.

Verbal Delivery

Besides being greatly conscious of your **visual** delivery (you and your visual aids) and **vocal** delivery (your manner of speaking), the audience will focus on your **verbal** delivery (the language you use and the way you construct sentences). Listeners prefer speakers who use a more informal language than what is usual for written reports. For instance, in oral speech, it is more appropriate to use short, simple sentences, and it is not always required to use complete sentences. Moreover, it is absolutely acceptable to use personal pronouns such as *I, we, you,* and *us* and contractions such as *I'm* and *don't* – forms that are frequently avoided in formal written reports.

One mistake is to use long or extremely technical terms or jargon to impress the audience. Even though you are speaking in a professional setting, don't think that your listeners use or understand the same technical words that you do. The best language is *vivid and colorful* (paints a picture for the audience), *concrete and specific* (gives details), and *simple* (is easy to understand).

Putting your ideas into simple, easy-to-understand language that suits the context of your audience and is vivid and specific, can be difficult at the start. As you practice on the essentials of delivery, remember the rules discussed here and your language and style of speaking will progress.

Methods of Delivery

There are four methods of delivering a speech: impromptu, manuscript reading, memorization, and extemporaneous.

1. The Impromptu Speech

Of the four methods, the impromptu speech requires the least preparation. With very little advance notice, the speaker is asked to speak for a few minutes on a specific subject.

Apply the following principles or rules in giving an impromptu speech:

- Formulate the central idea. Don't try to discuss the entire subject. Limit yourself to a specific aspect that you can discuss in a few minutes. *Be sure you know the idea you want to present before you start.*
- Open your talk with a sentence that says something. Don't be apologetic. Begin with a bang, and go straight to the point.
- The body of your speech must be unified. You can give examples, illustrations, comparisons, and contrasts to help explain your key sentences. Be as concrete and specific as possible.
- Conclude on a strong note. You can repeat your key sentences, but rephrase them. Restate them briefly but clearly.

Here are other guidelines with regards to giving an impromptu speech:

- Expect the possibility that you might be called on to speak, so make some preparations early. Understand what is being discussed, and create some relevant talking points on paper.

- Maximize whatever small amount of preparation time you are given to your benefit. Make an effort to think through what you want to say and rehearse it in your head as you are waiting to speak.

- Practice active listening. When you pay attention to what is being said, you will be able to create talking points for your presentation.

- Manage speech anxiety by reminding yourself that no one expects you to be perfect when you are asked to give impromptu speeches. Relax as much as possible, breathe slowly and don't be afraid to reference your notes to help you keep focused and on track.

- Use the fundamental principles of speech organization. Recall what I wrote earlier; tell them what you are going to tell them, tell them, and then tell them what you told them.

- Consider the impromptu speech as giving a golden opportunity to practice and develop your delivery. It is a great opportunity to develop your presentation skills, as it teaches you to focus on the moment, and trains you to think on your feet.

2. The Manuscript Speech

A manuscript or read speech is one that is written out and read word for word during delivery. When the occasion is a solemn or historic one, the read speech is the most appropriate. Persons of prominence read their speeches for accuracy and precision. This kind of speech lacks spontaneity and naturalness that the impromptu speech or the extemporaneous speech has. The speaker reading the speech should intensify their efforts to maintain rapport with the audience, as the manuscript speech can have the effect of boring an audience if it is delivered in a monotone by someone standing behind a podium.

Here are some guidelines in giving a manuscript speech:

- **Use a manuscript for the right reasons.** Does your speech have to be scripted, or can it be more impromptu?

- **Use good oral style.** Choose words and phrasing that will be readily understood by your audience.
- **Practice intensively.** This will help your delivery seem more natural and less scripted.
- **Look for opportunities to move and gesture.** Don't just stand and grip the podium.
- **Use your voice effectively.** Modulate your tone and volume to suit the script.
- **Remain flexible.** Adjust to the audience's response to your speech.

3. The Memorized Speech

This method of delivery is good only for elocution pieces. Like the manuscripted speech, it lacks spontaneity and naturalness. In addition, human memory might fail the speaker during the delivery and can cause great embarrassment.

Here are some guidelines in giving a memorized speech:

- Stay focused on your specific purpose and on the key ideas you want to convey.
- Speak in the moment; avoid thinking too far ahead in the speech.
- Practice, practice, practice!

4. The Extemporaneous Speech

This method is recommended for public speaking classes. It is not read nor memorized. It has spontaneity and naturalness. The speaker also has time to prepare the ideas embodied in it, though the language is formulated at the moment of delivery. This speech is also practiced but the words and arrangement of words are changed to something better and more effective. In rehearsing, the speaker is simply guided by a mental outline. If notes are held, these simply contain quotations from famous authors and speakers that help expound the ideas. The speaker doesn't memorize the speech but knows from memory the order of ideas to achieve unity, organization, and clarity in speech.

An extemporaneous speech:

- Requires careful preparation and research.
- Is based on a key word outline.
- Allows the speaker to remain direct, involved, and flexible.

Practicing Your Speech

"It's quite simple. Say what you have to say and when you come to a sentence with a grammatical ending, sit down."
Winston Churchill

At times, most speakers read through the outline silently a few times and think they are all set for a delivery. Nothing could be further from the truth. If you have not practiced your speech aloud several times, most likely you are not prepared to speak. There is a great difference between reading about how to deliver an effective speech and actually doing it. The only way to convert what you have read into what you can do is to *practice* it. Keep in mind that your objective is to sound confident and be natural – just like talking to friends. If you have been envisioning yourself giving a successful speech, you have taken a crucial first move towards confident delivery. Good or bad speeches are a matter of habit. Habits are formed and developed through constant practice.

Feeling confident while speaking is one of the advantages of practicing. The best outcomes are achieved if you prepare in two ways:

1. By envisioning yourself giving an effective and successful speech.
2. By actually practicing your speech aloud.

Here are pointers when practicing your speech:

- First, read through your speech silently several times until you are ready to begin.

- Practice delivering your speech aloud with your notes and outline. There is no alternative for practicing out loud. By standing on your feet, using your notes and visual aids, practicing your gestures and eye contact, and speaking aloud you are creating your presentation.

- Stand if possible before a full-length mirror. This will enable you to observe yourself as you speak. You will see yourself as the audience will see you.

- For the first rehearsals, use your outline until you are sure of your main points and their order.

- After the first rehearsal, pause and ask yourself if the order you followed is the best order of ideas possible, if the material you gathered is enough, if the way you expressed your ideas is the best, and if your choice of words is appropriate.

- Practice your speech aloud all the way through – noting parts that are rough, rereading your notes, and then practicing once more.

- Divide the speech into parts and practice major sections, such as the introduction, several times repeatedly.

- Repeat the practice session as many times as needed until you have gained self-confidence and self-assurance, taking note of the proper enunciation and pronunciation of your vowels and consonants, appropriate pausing and phrasing, stress, optimum pitch, and volume.
- When you are reasonably sure of your major headings and subtopics and their order, you may set aside your outline and practice with only your notes.
- Always take breaks. Avoid practicing so much at one time that you begin to lose your energy, voice, or concentration.
- Practice alone at first. Record (either audio or video) your speech and play it back in order to get feedback on your vocal delivery. Avoid dissecting your delivery. Concentrate on major concerns.
- If possible, visit the room where you will speak and practice using the equipment there, or practice in a room similar to the one in which you will be speaking. If your practice room does not have the equipment necessary for using your visuals, simulate handling them. If you are giving a manuscript speech, make sure that the manuscript is double or triple-spaced in 14 or 16-point type, this will make it much easier to read

at a glance. Place manuscript pages into a stiff binder. Practice holding the binder high enough that you can glance down at the manuscript without having to bob your head; few things annoy me more as an audience member then watching someone deliver a speech with their head going up and down like a bobblehead doll!

- When you begin to feel comfortable with your speech, practice in front of a small audience (friends or family members). Ask them for specific comments and feedback on your verbal, visual, and vocal delivery. Practice making direct eye contact and using gestures. If you have a video camera, let a friend film you so that you can observe yourself. Having a friend help is a good way to get you used to the idea of speaking in front of someone. If you discover any awkward spots in your speech (and you likely will), you can decide how to modify the speech to smooth them out.

- Over a period of time, practice your speech over again several times, all the way through, but guard against memorization. Note that practice doesn't mean memorize.

- Make sure to time yourself several times. If your speech is too long, make appropriate cuts. For example, you might cut a portion that is less important, use fewer illustrations, edit long quotations, or plan to tell the audience that you will be glad to address an issue more fully during the question-and-answer period. Note that if your speech is too long or too short, you may violate the audience's expectations and damage your credibility.

- At least once before the actual speech (two or three times would be better), practice using your visual aids with all the needed equipment. Again, it is critical to videotape yourself if possible, or ask a friend to observe one of your final practices.

- Try to get enough sleep the night before your speech. On the day of the speech, get to the venue early so that you can compose yourself. Check to see that your notes and visuals are in the proper order, and read through your outline one last time.

Bear in mind that no one expects you to be perfect. If you commit a mistake, correct it if necessary and proceed. Then forget it. If you have practiced until you feel comfortable with your speech and have envisioned yourself giving an effective speech, you should feel enthusiastic and confident.

Response to Audience Questions

The key to successful question-and-answer periods is to actually know your topic and expect questions from the audience. I actively encourage the audience to ask questions, because I know I will learn from their questions exactly how well I have done it delivering my message. One of the most frustrating things about speaking is the need to eliminate so much vital information (both personal and research-based) from your speech because of time constraints, so it's possible you can use the Q & A session to expand on your presentation.

Besides knowing your topic, expect several questions that you think your audience may ask and prepare one or two visual aids to use when answering these questions. Before preparing entirely new visuals, see if one or more overlays (for instance, one with a line graph that contains new information) could be included to a visual that you want to use in your speech. The overlays would be used only during the question-and-answer period. Certainly, it's always possible that none of these questions will be asked. But just in case, you can impress your audience tremendously.

The following suggestions may help you with your question-and-answer period. If you conduct audience questions well, you can make your message more convincing.

- Listen attentively to each question asked.

- Repeat & rephrase any confusing or negative questions in a clear and positive way. For example, "so if I understand your question, you are asking if your taxes will go up with this development I am proposing"

- Think a moment before answering each question. If you don't know the answer, say so, and refer the questioner to someone in the audience who does know. Or, tell the person that it's a good question and that you will find the answer and let that person know at the next meeting, or via a call or email.

- Do not allow one person to dominate the question period. When there are other people with their hands up, or at the microphone behind the person who is trying to dominate the question period, I politely point out to this person that I would like to give as many people as possible the opportunity to ask questions.

- If you think a question is irrelevant or will take too long to answer, thank the person for the question and mention that it could be a complex question to answer in the time you have, and you will be pleased talk with that individual personally about it after the question period.

- Don't try to fake your way through a response. If you don't know, admit it. NOTHING will destroy your credibility quicker than trying to bluff or lie your way through a question.

- Don't argue or get angry or defensive while answering questions. What you say during the question-and-answer period will influence the audience's overall judgment of your credibility and your speech.

- If appropriate, actively encourage listeners to participate. I use a line such as "I know with all this information I have given that there must be a point I can expand on; can anyone tell me what they would like to have further clarification on?"

- If you expect a very hostile audience, try to avoid a question-and-answer period. If this is not possible, mention in your introduction that there will be a short question-and-answer period at the end of your speech and ask the audience to write out questions during the speech. After your initial conclusion, collect the questions, select three or four good ones, and answer them – ignoring the less desirable ones.

- Watch your time, and end the period with a final conclusion that refocuses audience attention, leads them to the outcome that you desire, and puts a pleasing closure on your speech.

12

COMMONLY ASKED QUESTIONS

"The one real object of education is to have a man in the condition of continually asking questions."

Bishop Mandell Creighton

Q: How do I manage fear, apprehension, stage fright, and speech anxiety?

A: Gradually, and with focused practice. These are very common issues even for experienced speakers. Increased nervousness and rapid heartbeat before a speech are the coping mechanisms of the body. The more experienced you become, the better prepared you will be; the better prepared you are, the calmer you will be. Every one of us experiences these apprehensions, so it is good to breathe out the accumulated carbon dioxide in your lungs and breathe deeply before you begin your speech. Beginning your speech slowly helps decrease nervousness, and actually causes the audience to pay attention.

Q: How do I capture and maintain the listener's attention and interest?

A: Remember the following:

- Establish eye contact with the audience.
- Make appropriate pauses for the audience to process what you are saying.
- Use interesting and powerful visual aids.
- Talk from personal experience and tell stories.
- Make your speech concise and to the point. Don't use a ten dollar word when a one dollar word will do.

Q: How do I know when the listeners are bored and inattentive?

A: Observe the following:

- A lot of listeners sit with their arms folded.
- Vacant looks – no smiles or nodding of the head.
- Murmurs of conversation.
- Most of the people are yawning.
- Polite coughs which are more than usual.
- Nonverbal gestures like audience frequently looking at their watches, biting their nails,

shuffling their feet, looking at each other, and worse, starting to exit the venue.

Q: How do I develop my self-confidence?

A: Practice, practice, practice is the key. Look for every chance to give a speech. The more you face the audience, the more you will develop self-confidence. Begin with very short speeches that last three to four minutes. Always bear in mind that a short speech can barely go wrong. Impromptu speeches make good practice. Concentrate and be natural. Do not try to pretend to be someone else, your audience will see right through this. Master your topic; do careful research and double check your facts. Believe in yourself, and believe me when I say that everyone that you see and admire that speaks publicly has been nervous about the experience at some point in their lives. It is critical that you know and understand this, because it will help you see that you can grow and develop your skills as a speaker. It just takes practice and a desire to succeed. If you don't believe in yourself, trust me, no one else will.

Q: How much information must I gather for a speech?

A: Your experience is your guide. Some need 60 minutes of information for a 5-minute speech. Some will have to read extensively to prepare. At times you have to conduct very little research. The most important information source is typically drawn from your personal experience with the topic at hand. There's an old saying that I quote when I teach: "you know when you know". You will know when you have gathered enough information to deliver a presentation that will meet your audience's expectations.

Q: Can I memorize a speech?

A: Yes, you can. But don't. Never memorize a speech. You are bound to miss out a line or two and worse, your speech will likely be insincere. When I watch someone who has memorized a speech, I often have the thought that they are standing there on stage reading aloud a script in their mind....you can practically see the pages turning! When you do this, your listeners will discover almost instantly what you are doing, because memorizing stops you from being natural. If you like, you could memorize a specific poem or a memorable quote to interject at the appropriate time in your presentation.

Q: Can I read a speech?

A: Yes, you can. But don't. That is the best technique to bore a listener, and this is one of the main reasons that political speeches are so dry. The only instance you read a speech is when you do it on behalf of someone else. Even when you do that, make it brief or summarize it. At the end of the summary, you can give out the entire speech in the form of a handout. This will help the audience absorb your words. The written language and the spoken language are different forms of expression, so what is beautifully written may not sound beautiful when it is spoken.

Q: Can I use notes during a speech?

A: Yes, you can. But be sure that they don't appear bulky. The worst thing a speaker can do is to pull out pages and pages of notes before a speech. Whenever I see this I listen for the inevitable groan from the audience, because they believe that they are about to be bored to tears! Having said that, preparing 3 x 5 index cards is all right. Be sure your entire speech does not go beyond seven cards. A single sheet of paper with an outline of your speech is still the best. Be sure the letters on that single sheet are big enough to read. I suggest a minimum font of 14-18 points, in bold typeface.

Q: How do I develop my speech?

A: Never talk about one idea too long. If you have three ideas, allot equal time to each, and make the transition from one idea to the next smooth. Listeners must not wait too long for the next idea. If you dwell too long on one idea, it is inevitable that the audience will become bored, and you will struggle to maintain control of the message.

Q: During an open forum, what do I do when a person gives a speech rather than asking a question?

A: Typically open forums are specific meetings or events. By my experience an open forum is intended to be an event in which people can gather to find out about a specific issue, and hear from several speakers on the topic or topics. Although an open forum is intended to be a space in which free speech is encouraged, you will encounter people who will have a private agenda, and attempt to dominate the event. When I am hosting a public forum I remind people that they are expected to behave politely, and although they are welcome to disagree with each other, that time must be made for all to give voice to their ideas and thoughts. The best way to do this is limit speakers to a certain amount of time, and politely enforce this rule. It is your responsibility as moderator or host to interrupt and say, "Excuse me, what exactly is your question?" Use the summary technique I gave you earlier;

"So if I understand your question, you are saying….." Do not let someone try to take control of the question period; you will cause the rest of the audience to lose respect for you. If the question is too long or the response too complicated for the allotted time, ask the person to meet with you after the question period ends and you will answer their question.

Q: What do I do when I get a hostile question?

A: Be cool. Be courteous and if they are wrong, disagree with a smile by saying, "Perhaps I was not clear." or "It's possible you misunderstood." Once you have covered a topic as thoroughly as you planned to, you could end the discussion by saying that "you have explained your position, and out of respect for everyone's time it is time to move on." To appease the audience, you can offer to discuss the issue further after you conclude your presentation.

Q: How do I handle a hostile audience?

A: By my experience, most audiences are supportive and open to what you have to say. Still, the time is bound to come when you will have to face an audience who are openly resistant or even hostile. But rest assured, there are ways to deal with the problem. Almost always, you'll know in advance that you'll be dealing with a hostile audience. If you have done your homework it should not come as a surprise, and when it does, it's usually the result of poor preparation for the event. So, *before* you present, make sure you've done your audience analysis. I encourage you to go to my website at **www.speakandwin.com** to download the free audience analysis template. I know you will find it to be very helpful. By following a few simple steps you can do alot to minimize and even prevent adverse audience reaction by anticipating how your listeners are likely to react to what you say.

Q: What do I do when someone has many questions in one question?

A: Answer them one by one and begin with the easiest. Again, you can use the summary tool I gave you and modify your response by saying "I see several questions within your question; let's break it down so everyone can understand". Then proceed to answer each question, in context to the main question, which you can refer back to.

And In Conclusion

Take time out to listen to as many speeches as possible. A good listener is a successful communicator. Don't forget to take down notes when you listen to these speeches. Recognize speeches that you like and those you can't stand. Examine the speeches you like, and there you will learn useful and helpful tips to develop your speech. Examine the speeches you dislike, and there you will learn what you should avoid doing. I know that by using the methods I have taught you in this book that you will not only learn to control your fear of public speaking, but you will begin to turn that fear into excitement!

One of the things I hope you have taken from this book is that it is not just a book about Public Speaking; it is also a book about creating leadership. Consider how you can craft your words to have a positive impact not only on your life, but on the lives of others around you. Consider the rich history of mankind, and how the words of some decidedly common people have had a profound impact on all of our lives.

But please remember what you have read here are just words if you do not take action on what you have learned.

My wish for you is that my words will lead you to prosperity, and that you share your gifts with others; when you do this you will have truly learned to

Speak and Win!

"Live as if you were to die tomorrow. Learn as if you were to live forever."

Mohandas Gandhi

14660595R00076

Made in the USA
Charleston, SC
24 September 2012